LET GOD
SURPRISE YOU

LET GOD SURPRISE YOU

TRUST GOD *with* YOUR DREAMS

HEATHER WHITESTONE MCCALLUM
and ANGELA HUNT

ZONDERVAN™

GRAND RAPIDS, MICHIGAN 49530 USA

We want to hear from you. Please send your comments about this book to us in care of zreview@zondervan.com. Thank you.

ZONDERVAN™

Let God Surprise You
Copyright © 2003 by Heather Whitestone McCallum and Angela Elwell Hunt

Requests for information should be addressed to:

Zondervan, *Grand Rapids, Michigan 49530*

Library of Congress Cataloging-in-Publication Data

Whitestone-McCallum, Heather
  Let God surprise you : trust God with your dreams / Heather Whitestone-McCallum and Angela Hunt.
    p. cm.
  Includes bibliographical references.
  ISBN 0-310-24628-8
  1. Trust in God. 2. Whitestone-McCallum, Heather. I. Hunt, Angela Elwell, 1957– II. Title.
  BV4637 .W48 2003
  248.8'43—dc21

                                                          2003002410

Published in association with the literary agency of Alive Communications, Inc., 7680 Goddard Street, Suite 200, Colorado Springs, CO 80920.

Interior design by Todd Sprague

Printed in the United States of America

---

04 05 06 07/❖ DC/ 10 9 8 7 6 5 4 3

*For my beloved sons and
all the children of the world
including those with disabilities
May God bless you with his dreams*

CONTENTS

INTRODUCTION

WHEN I WAS FIVE YEARS OLD, GOD GAVE ME THE DESIRE TO become a famous ballerina. Many little girls have this dream, but most of them aren't deaf.

I have suffered from deafness since the autumn of 1974. On a September day when I was eighteen months old, I awakened with a slight fever. My mother, who had nursed my two older sisters through various childhood illnesses, wasn't overly concerned at first. But as my fever soared above 104 degrees, she realized we were facing a life-or-death situation.

In an effort to bring my fever down, my doctors gave me two strong antibiotics with risky side effects. Those medications saved my life, but they also took their toll on my young body.

On Christmas Day that year, circumstances proved that I would be forever different. As my mother hurried about preparing the traditional holiday dinner, she opened a kitchen cabinet and spilled a stack of pots and pans. Everyone in the living room jumped. My grandmother, who had been watching me play by the Christmas tree, anxiously called Mother into the living room.

"Daphne," she said, peering at me. "I think there's something wrong with Heather's hearing."

My mother rushed back into the kitchen to grab a pan and a wooden spoon. As she stood behind me and drowned out the Christmas carols on the stereo with her frantic banging and clanging, I kept playing with my toys. I had no idea she was there.

After a series of tests, the doctors told my parents I was profoundly deaf. They predicted I would not develop much verbal speech. They said I would probably not acquire knowledge beyond a third-grade education.

Tests revealed that I had at least a 120-decibel hearing loss in my right ear and a 90-decibel hearing loss in my left—and that's when I'm wearing my hearing aid. Without it I hear nothing from either ear.

Through my childhood years I worked hard to develop speech and learn how to read lips, but I also found a place of escape from the rigors of hard work. That place was, strangely enough, the Dothan School of Dance. My instructor, Patti Rutland, had faith in me and in my dream of becoming a ballerina.

My collaborator, Angela Hunt, has written a best-selling book called *The Tale of Three Trees*. I love this old folktale because it illustrates how God longs to make our dreams come true, but often he brings our dreams to us in surprising ways.

In her version of the three trees story, the first tree longed to be a treasure chest, the second tree yearned to sail mighty waters, and the third tree wanted to point men to God. When three woodcutters climbed the mountain, all three trees waited anxiously to see how God would bring their dreams to pass.

The first tree was disappointed when the carpenter fashioned him into a humble manger—until Mary placed her baby within his embrace and he realized he was holding the greatest treasure in the world.

The second tree was heartbroken when the carpenter pounded him into a simple fishing boat—until Jesus calmed the storm from his bow and he realized he was carrying the king of heaven and earth.

The third tree despaired when she found herself being used as the cross in Christ's crucifixion—until the power of God raised Jesus from the dead. Then she realized that every time men thought of her, they would think of God.

Yes, God made their dreams come true—after he had led them through the valleys of testing and trial. God made my dreams come true, but I walked through those same valleys. Learning how to speak and read lips required hard work; learning how to dance required discipline and long stretches of practice.

But hard work wasn't the only ingredient in my success. As a young woman I learned that God loves to surprise his children in the way he works out the plans he has for us, the dreams he has planted in our spirits. He loves to do the unexpected, even the outrageous. His incredible wonders give us an opportunity to witness for Jesus and glorify him more. I love receiving surprises from God because he always amazes me. I have learned that we really can do all things through Jesus Christ and his strength.

Don't be discouraged when it seems as if your dreams are no more substantial than tattered cobwebs. Keep your head up and meditate on God's Word.

I wrote this book because I wanted to share the things I've learned—and I began to learn them in the solitude of my room, where I would hold my Bible on my lap and read. God's Word is a lamp for our feet, a light that will illuminate the way ahead. Sometimes its direction is clear exhortation, but I also value and have learned so much from the characters who play out the biblical story line.

Here I want to share with you some of the lessons I see in the lives of significant biblical characters. Except for our Lord, they were not perfect men and women, yet their journeys show how God used them and their dreams in surprising ways, for his good and theirs. I also share the stories of more recent historical or contemporary believers who have changed their world as they worked to fulfill their dreams.

Come with me now as we look at stories of people who chose to believe—and were surprised by this outrageous, outlandish, and loving God we serve.

one

SURPRISED BY BIG DREAMS

THE STORY OF JOSEPH, SON OF JACOB, IS ONE OF MY FAVORITE Bible stories. Like me, Joseph was a dreamer. While some of his dreams of his future role came as memorable messages as he slept, my dreams of becoming a famous ballerina sprang from my heart's desires. Before I take you to Joseph's world in ancient Canaan and Egypt, I'd like to give you a glimpse of mine as a child and teenager full of big dreams.

MY DREAM

It is difficult to remember much about my early years, but I do remember dreaming of being a ballerina. Because I was profoundly deaf, I spent much of my childhood in speech therapy, which I quickly learned to dread. Speech therapy was hard work, even for a five year old.

The summer before I entered kindergarten, God gave my mother the idea of enrolling me in a dance class. She had noticed that I enjoyed music in my listening therapy classes, so she thought that music might help me better understand the pitch and tone that are a part of natural speech.

Trouble was, not many dance classes were eager to accept a profoundly deaf student. Mother called two dance studios before she found one that would accept me. Patti Richards, a teacher at the Dothan School of Dance, was willing to take a chance, and I fell in love with her immediately. While ballet is a lot of hard work, I took to it like a duck to water. It was sheer fun, and soon I was twirling my way around our house. Even at that young age, I dreamed of dancing for God.

I didn't yet understand what it meant to have a personal relationship with Christ, but I knew God made the world and I could sense his love for me. And somehow I felt that nothing could please him more than seeing me exercise the gift he had given me—a love for dance.

Becoming a ballerina was my dream, and as I grew older I became determined not to let anybody take it away. Young life is like a blank page, full of opportunity, but too many children listen to naysayers and do not have confidence in their own aspirations. When children are told they can't do something, they often stop trying. But we all have a right to dream—and to follow those dreams.

As I grew older, however, I began to realize that dreams have to exist alongside reality. I wanted to dance, but I needed an education. After graduating from high school, I would have given anything to forget about college and join a ballet company, but I knew my education was important. My parents kept pushing me toward college, but truly great ballerinas enter a ballet company in their mid-teens. I was told dancing could wait, but it couldn't, not really. A dancer's prime is a fleeting thing, and young dancers must begin early and train hard. How could I do both?

Even though I couldn't see how I could possibly complete my education and achieve my dream, I clung even more tightly to my vision of dancing before millions. And since God had given me the dream of dancing, I believed he would make a way for it to come true.

The Bible tells us about another young dreamer, Joseph. His dream must have seemed impossible when God first sent it to him, but our God delights in doing the impossible.

JOSEPH'S JOURNEY

The book of Genesis goes into great detail telling Joseph's long story, from his nomadic childhood to his prominent post as Pharaoh's main man. As a boy he had a sense of God's great plans for him, revealed in dreams. He related these dreams to his brothers, who were already a bit envious of him because he was their father's favorite:

> "Listen to this dream I had: We were binding sheaves of grain out in the field when suddenly my

sheaf rose and stood upright, while your sheaves gathered around mine and bowed down to it."

His brothers said to him, "Do you intend to reign over us? Will you actually rule us?" And they hated him all the more because of his dream and what he had said (Gen. 37:6–8).

That was the first dream. Then there was a second:

"Listen," he said, "I had another dream, and this time the sun and moon and eleven stars were bowing down to me."

When he told his father as well as his brothers, his father rebuked him and said, "What is this dream you had? Will your mother and I and your brothers actually come and bow down to the ground before you?" (Gen. 37:9–10)

Poor Joseph! His envious brothers didn't respond well to his tales. I believe Joseph knew his vision had originated with the Spirit of God, but it's obvious his brothers didn't think so! Neither did Jacob, his father.

Still, Joseph carried his dream within him, like a seed, and waited to see how it would grow. I'm sure the memory of this dream gave Joseph courage and comfort during his dark days of testing and trial.

You may remember that Joseph's journey to greatness was long and arduous. His envious brothers sold him to slave traders who took him to Egypt. Far from home, he must have been tempted to forget his father's God and everything he had ever learned about holiness. It would have been easy for him to become angry and blame God for the desperate straits he was in. He could have mentally divorced himself from his people, his past, and his purpose in life.

But Joseph did not give into those temptations. Observing his integrity and talents, and sensing that "the Lord was with [him]" (Gen. 39:2), his master, Potiphar, placed Joseph in charge of his household. But that was not the end of the story. That chapter ends with Joseph being sent to prison, falsely accused of attempted rape when he refused to sleep with Potiphar's wife. But even there, Joseph did not lose sight of his dream of leadership. The prison warden, seeing his potential and his heart for God, placed him in charge of other inmates. "The Lord was with Joseph and gave him success in whatever he did" (Gen. 39:23).

In that dark prison, God was working on his biggest surprise yet, connecting Joseph to a man who would eventually introduce him to Pharaoh. One thing led to another and in time God elevated Joseph to the second-highest position in Egypt. Through Joseph, God revealed that the current national prosperity would be followed by a great famine. Joseph presented a plan to stockpile grain that fed the Egyptians and most of the Middle East for seven years.

But even after being promoted to this prominent position, Joseph did not forget the God who had brought him to this place. Neither did he forget to do right.

One day Joseph's brothers arrived at the palace, asking Joseph for food. He not only fed them, but he also invited them all to Egypt to live. Years later, when their father died, they worried that he would strike out at them for the terrible things they had done to him. The brothers sent a message to Joseph that contained a request from their father: "I ask you to forgive your brothers the sins and the wrongs they committed in treating you so badly" (Gen. 50:17).

When the brothers came directly to Joseph, they couldn't imagine that he would show them mercy. Reminiscent of Joseph's childhood dreams, the brothers bowed down before him and offered themselves to his service:

> "We are your slaves," they said.
>   But Joseph said to them, "Don't be afraid. Am I in the place of God? You intended to harm me, but God intended it for good to accomplish what is now being done, the saving of many lives. So then, don't be afraid. I will provide for you and your children." And he reassured them and spoke kindly to them (Gen. 50:18–21).

In Joseph's story I see a godly pattern for life. He had integrity, being honest in his business practices and resisting sexual temptation, and he did not repay evil for evil. Most important, he honored God above the praise of men. This is so clear in the great line "Am I in the place of God?" He never knew how God's plan for him would be fulfilled, but he could see that God could use any obstacle to further God's good plan—for Joseph himself and for the wider community.

TRUST, ACKNOWLEDGE, AND OBEY

Joseph did not have the written Scriptures at hand. But if he had, he was the kind of person who would have memorized Proverbs 3:5–6:

> Trust in the Lord with all your heart
> and lean not on your own understanding;
> in all your ways acknowledge him,
> and he will make your paths straight.

I have learned not to rely on my understanding alone. That's not to say I don't *use* my understanding, I just don't *rely* on it.

In high school, I encountered another bump in the road—my parents divorced. The house became very quiet when Dad moved out, and during those hours I began to want to know more about God. The more I learned about Jesus, the more I wanted to learn about him. So I began to study his word. I thought I could please God by being a good girl and doing good things. I thought if I was good enough, God would accept me. I tried to follow his commandments—and found that task a lot harder than I expected.

I remember praying a lot about my parents' break up. I actually went as far as to tell my mother that God doesn't like divorce, and she turned away, not pleased with the idea of her daughter preaching to her. That's when I realized that my dream of a reconciliation between my parents would not come true. But though I ached inside, God spoke to my heart and comforted me just like he comforts everyone who turns to him when a cherished dream vanishes like breath upon a mirror.

Yet God loves to bring good out of tragedy. Because my heart was hurting, I spent hours in God's Word, searching for wisdom in the Scripture. I read that God wants children to obey their parents—whether they're together or not. As I prepared for college, it was clear that my parents wanted me to go to Jacksonville State University—a school without a ballet class. Their decision left me feeling confused. How could I fulfill my God-given dream if I couldn't study dance or audition for a ballet company?

I spent a long time praying about my decision, and I knew I had to obey God's Word. So I chose to listen to my parents and see how God would work to fulfill the dream he had planted in my heart. I trusted him with my future. I trusted that he, like a good gardener, would take care of his flowers—in this case, me and the dream he had planted in my heart.

Jacksonville State University provided the help I needed for college, but my journey to Atlantic City really began the year before I arrived at JSU. While still a senior in high school, I visited the college and went to the recruiting office to meet someone who would show me around the campus. When I stepped into the office, I was struck by the pictures of four pretty young women on the walls. The receptionist saw my glance and told me that the women were JSU students who had gone on to win Miss Alabama. "That one," she said, pointing to a beautiful woman's portrait, "is Teresa Strickland, who you're waiting to meet. She not only won Miss Alabama, but went on to become first runner-up in the 1979 Miss America pageant."

Wow, she's so beautiful! I thought. *This woman is really something.* Teresa Cheatham Strickland looked like a model when she stepped out to meet me, and I couldn't believe she was willing to introduce me to JSU. I was immediately impressed by her humble attitude. Though beautiful and charming, she seemed so peaceful and kind.

As I look back on it, enrolling at Jacksonville was a little like Joseph going to Egypt, where he made connections God would later use for his purposes. Teresa Strickland's example and faith in God guided me as I participated in pageants. A few years later I found myself dancing as Miss Alabama on a national television show watched by more than forty million people.

My dream had come true—in a way I never would have predicted.

One of my favorite scriptural promises appears in Jeremiah 29:11: "'For I know the plans I have for you,' declares the Lord, 'plans to prosper you and not to harm you, plans to give you hope and a future.'"

This reminds me that God has a wonderful and unique plan for each person on earth. Our plans become clear as we seek God, who implants dreams and then reveals his plans as we trust him with one step at a time.

GOD, PLEASE SHOW ME ...

The life story of George Washington Carver inspires me to continue to trust God and acknowledge his role in my dreams-come-true. This African American man, born of slave parents in Missouri, became a confidant and advisor to leaders and scientists around the world: Thomas Edison, Mahatma Gandhi, Calvin Coolidge, and Franklin Roosevelt. Like Joseph, he rose from obscurity to a position of tremendous influence. Who was Carver, and why did so many important men seek his advice?

As a boy Carver took a great interest in nature—plants and rocks. He learned their names, studied their characteristics, and earned a reputation for being a "plant doctor." After working his way through college, he used his knowledge and his concern for the southern states to revitalize its agricultural economy.

As an agricultural chemist, he found three hundred uses for the peanut, more than a hundred uses for sweet potatoes, and seventy-five for pecans. He discovered new ways to make face powder, lotion, shaving cream, vinegar, cold cream, printer's ink, salad oil, rubbing oil, instant coffee, leather stains, synthetic tapioca and egg yolk, flour, paints, and non-toxic colors. He developed a new type of cotton, known as Carver's hybrid.

The big surprise in Carver's story is that he never carried science textbooks or publications into his laboratory, only the Bible. He once told a church group,

> God is going to reveal to us things He never revealed before if we put our hands in His. No books ever go into my laboratory. The thing I am to do and the way of doing it are revealed to me. I never have to grope for methods. The method is revealed to me the moment I am inspired to create something new. Without God to draw aside the curtain I would be helpless. . . . Only alone can I draw close enough to God to discover His secrets.[1]

In the summer of 1920 Carver spoke at a meeting of the Young Men's Christian Association of Blue Ridge,

North Carolina. His approach to science surprised many in his audience. He said,

> Years ago I went into my laboratory and said, "Dear Mr. Creator, please tell me what the universe was made for?"
>
> The Great Creator answered, "You want to know too much for that little mind of yours. Ask for something more your size, little man."
>
> Then I asked, "Please, Mr. Creator, tell me what man was made for?"
>
> Again the Great Creator replied, "You are still thinking too much. Cut down on the extent and improve the intent."
>
> So then I asked, "Please, Mr. Creator, will you tell me why the peanut was made?"
>
> "That's better, but even then it's infinite. What do you want to know about the peanut?"
>
> "Mr. Creator, can I make milk out of the peanut?"
>
> "What kind of milk do you want? Good Jersey milk or just plain boarding house milk?"
>
> "Good Jersey milk."
>
> And then the Great Creator taught me to take the peanut apart and put it together again. And out of the process have come forth all these products![2]

In 1921, Carver went to Washington to address the U.S. Senate Ways and Means Committee on the uses of the peanut and other new crops that could improve the South's economy. After listening to Carver's presentation, the committee chairman asked him how he had learned all this. Carver said,

"From an old book."

"What book?"

"The Bible."

The chairman smiled. "Does the Bible tell about peanuts?"

"No, sir," Dr. Carver replied, "but it tells about the God who made the peanut. I asked him to show me what to do with the peanut, and he did."[3]

Like Joseph, George Washington Carver honored God rather than pocketing praise. He could have easily allowed men to exalt him for his brilliant inventions and ideas, but he always gave credit to the great Creator. He saw himself as a coworker with God and saw this potential in everyone.

Sounds amazing, doesn't it? But you can be a coworker with God by having simple, childlike faith and listening for his voice. He is waiting for you to ask questions like Dr. Carver. He is waiting for you to ask him which step you should take next—and how you should approach that decision looming in your future. If he has given you a dream, he wants you to nourish and cherish it, even through days of testing and trial.

Let God surprise you. Like Joseph and George Washington Carver, decide that you will trust the Lord with your dreams and acknowledge him in all your ways.

"Delight yourself in the Lord and he will give you the desires of your heart" (Psalm 37:4).

two

SURPRISED
BY SIN

EVE'S LOST PERFECTION

Because I'm a former Miss America, you might think I'm a rabid follower of beauty pageants. If so, I hate to disappoint you, but I'm not. The world is filled with beautiful women, and I have always thought inner beauty is much more appealing than physical perfection.

But now I'm thinking of one woman who must have been the most perfect, the most physically beautiful woman ever created. If she were resurrected and entered in a beauty pageant along with Esther, Bathsheba, Sarah, and representatives from the current fifty states, I'm convinced she'd win with a unanimous vote of the judges. Who is this raving beauty? Eve, the mother of all who have ever lived.

Eve was the first woman ever created. God formed her when the earth was young and unsullied, before sin had an opportunity to cast its long shadow over her heart and her countenance. Eve was perfection itself—as lovely in form and face as she was in mind and spirit.

I am sure you recall the creation story found in the first chapters of Genesis. God created the world. He fashioned a beautiful garden. And he scooped up a handful of clay and breathed into it, creating the first man, Adam. God pronounced everything he made good, but regarding man, he said, "It is not good that man should be alone." So he caused a deep sleep to fall upon the man, and from the man's rib he took bone and blood and marrow and created woman.

You have probably heard the lovely lines by commentator Matthew Henry:

> This companion was taken from [Adam's] side to signify that she was to be dear unto him as his own flesh. Not from his head, lest she should rule over him; nor from his feet, lest he should tyrannize over her; but from his side, to denote that species of equality which is to subsist in the marriage state.[1]

And there you have a picture of bliss—a perfect man, a perfect woman, in a perfect garden. They were to have the perfect marriage and raise perfect children; but God, in his wisdom and mercy, didn't want perfect automatons. He wanted to fellowship with people who *chose* to love him, who followed him freely. So in the garden he placed a fruit tree and called it the tree of knowledge of good and evil. We don't know what kind of fruit this tree bore, only that the fruit looked delicious.

"You may eat of anything in the garden," God told Adam and Eve, "except the tree of knowledge of good and evil. In the day you eat from it, you shall surely die."

Adam and Eve, you see, were supposed to live forever in bodies that never aged or became sick. But everything changed one day when Eve took a solitary walk and paused by the forbidden tree. There she met Satan in the form of a serpent.

> Now the serpent was more crafty than any of the wild animals the Lord God had made. He said to the woman, "Did God really say, 'You must not eat from any tree in the garden'?"
>
> The woman said to the serpent, "We may eat fruit from the trees in the garden, but God did say, 'You must not eat fruit from the tree that is in the middle of the garden, and you must not touch it, or you will die.'"
>
> "You will not surely die," the serpent said to the woman. "For God knows that when you eat of it your eyes will be opened, and you will be like God, knowing good and evil" (Gen. 3:1–5).

Eve didn't expect to have a headlong encounter with sin on her afternoon walk; as an innocent creation, she didn't even know what sin was. Until the moment of her temptation, she had used her free will to worship God, to enjoy fellowship with her husband, to choose what they would eat and where they would wander in the garden. She had undoubtedly made many choices since her creation, but now, for the first time, she considered doing something expressly against the will of God.

Yes, the serpent lied. He twisted the truth. God hadn't meant they'd die an immediate *physical* death if they ate, but a *spiritual* death, or separation from God. The serpent went on to compound his lie, promising that Eve would be like God if she ate.

Eve would never be as great or powerful or wise as God, but in one terrible way she would be like God if she ate the forbidden fruit. Like him, she would know the pain of separation and understand hurt. But unlike God, she would experience disobedience and suffer the taint of sin.

Eve knew disobeying was wrong. The last thing in the world she wanted to become was a sinner. But she wanted to taste that fruit. So she plucked the fruit and ate it, then gave some to Adam, who ate as well.

In that moment, innocence died. Eve's spirit shriveled. And when the Lord God went for a walk in the cool of the day (probably the Lord Jesus in one of his Old Testament appearances), he called out to Adam and Eve. When they heard his voice, instead of running toward him to enjoy his company, they hid in shame.

Sin corrupts everything. Whether a person plans to sin or sins impulsively, nothing will ever be the same.

No Silly Story

I vividly remember a day when I was about ten years old. I'm blushing as I tell this story because I'm not proud of it. But this particular afternoon changed my life and my perception of the world.

I was shopping with my dad and sisters in a neighborhood K-Mart. We scattered inside the store, each of us going to our favorite places. I went to the toy aisle and browsed for a bit, then spied a wonderful little egg filled with Silly Putty.

I don't know if you remember Silly Putty, but the TV commercials made it look like miracle stuff. You could take a ball of Silly Putty, apply it to the newspaper comics, then lift it up to find the comic images on the sticky clay. You could then stretch the images into all sorts of funny faces.

I knew I'd have lots of fun with Silly Putty and I wanted it desperately. I found my father and asked him to buy the Silly Putty egg, but he said no. I begged him; still, he refused. I could read his lips loud and clear—NO.

Then my dad and sisters moved into another aisle and I lingered in the toy section. I turned around and took a long look at the wonderful Silly Putty egg. Like Eve staring at that fruit tree, I looked at the egg and thought about how much enjoyment that little object would bring me.

I knew the difference between right and wrong. I knew stealing was very, very wrong. The last thing in the world I wanted to be was a thief.

But I wanted that little egg. So I picked it up and dropped it into my pocket.

When we arrived home, I went into the family room. As my family went about their business, I sat in a chair and tried to figure out how I was going to evade blame for my wrongdoing. I didn't mind taking the egg, but I sure didn't want to take the responsibility for what I had done.

So I put my hand in my pocket and widened my eyes. "Look, everybody," I said, acting for all I was worth. "I can't believe this fell into my pocket!"

I held up the egg of Silly Putty, certain my family would rejoice in my good fortune, but they weren't about to be taken in by my dramatics. My oldest sister, Stacy, mouthed her favorite words: "You are in *big* trouble."

My mother gave me a look that said she couldn't believe I thought she was stupid. And my father, who had heard me begging for the Silly Putty only a few minutes before, cut to the quick: "Heather Whitestone! You stole that toy."

My spirit shriveled just like Eve's. In front of my entire family, I had opened my heart and revealed my selfishness and sin.

My mother took me back to K-Mart. She marched me in to meet the cashier, where I was supposed to confess. As I stared down at my shoes, I could feel the pressure of dozens of pairs of eyes—we lived in a small town, and at that moment, I felt like the entire community was inside K-Mart, their eyes bearing down on me like searchlights.

Mother asked me to confess and to apologize to the cashier. As bad as I was feeling, you would think I would have had the sense to obey, but my pride hadn't been broken. I looked up and told her no.

Furious, Mother paid for the Silly Putty, then marched me back out to the car. I was certain I would get a spanking once we got home, but when we arrived, we discovered that a pipe had broken inside the house and the floor was flooded. Mother ran in to fight the flood and forgot about the Silly Putty. She may have forgotten, but I never did. I felt guilty for a long, long time.

Guilt is not always a bad thing. It serves a useful purpose, because it reminds us that we are not perfect, not holy, not deserving of heaven. Guilt reminds us that we require an intercessor. We need someone to step in and carry us across the gap between us and God. That's what Jesus does.

Guilt remained with me until the day I accepted Jesus Christ as my Savior. Stealing Silly Putty was just one sin; I had committed so many others. But Jesus forgave me and delivered me from the taint of sin just as he delivered Eve.

How did he deliver Eve? He promised that from her lineage would come a Savior who would redeem a world that had fallen into sin. I placed my faith in the Savior who appeared generations ago; Eve placed her faith in the Savior who would appear generations later.

That, I think, is the best news of all. Whenever we are surprised by sin—either ours or someone else's—that same Savior, Jesus Christ, stands willing to forgive.

NEVER TOO LATE

Steve Arterburn, founder of Women of Faith and New Life Clinics, has made a tremendous difference in the lives of countless women around the world. But years ago Steve was a man who, by his own admission, treated women with contempt. While in college, he paid for the abortion of his baby. He was sexually promiscuous and regarded women as objects to be desired, not people to be esteemed. So, what motivated this man to establish the largest traveling Christian women's conference in the United States?

In his book, *Flashpoints,* he writes:

> I am often asked why I think God chose me, a man, to begin Women of Faith. I don't fully know the answer to that question, but I do know that God can put the pieces of our life together like a jigsaw puzzle—the good, the bad, and the ugly—to make a beautiful picture. In my case, for years I had seen women as objects and treated them disdainfully. Over time, as God touched and healed some deep wounds in my life, my view of women began to change. Out of that healing came a desire to give something back to women, to atone for what I had taken.[2]

Steve is also a frequent speaker at pro-life rallies. There he shares his pain, his shame about the past, and the sense of loss he still feels. He also tells his audience about his adopted daughter, born of parents with the courage he did not possess while in college.

"I have to be honest," he says. "I've made some big mistakes in my life. But I've learned that it's never too late to change. It's never too late to find the life you desire."[3]

Yes, sin taints everything it touches, but through Jesus we can find the peace and courage we need to pick up the pieces and move forward. Eve did. I did. Steve did.

You can too.

three

SURPRISED BY
NEW FAITH

~

RUTH'S REDEMPTION

"Don't urge me to leave you or to turn back from you. Where you go I will go, and where you stay I will stay. Your people will be my people and your God my God" (Ruth 1:16).

The above quote is often recited at weddings; in fact, the minister repeated it in my own marriage ceremony. Few people, however, realize that those words did not originate with a married couple. They were first spoken by Ruth, a Gentile woman, to her mother-in-law, Naomi, from the Israelite tribe of Judah. Both women had lost their husbands. Both were alone in the world.

Ten years before, Naomi, her husband, and two sons had moved to Moab to flee a famine in and around their town of Bethlehem. While living in Moab, Naomi's sons married Moabite wives, Orpah and Ruth. Then tragedy struck—one by one, Naomi's husband and sons died, leaving three widows, all of them childless.

A short time later Naomi learned that the Lord had blessed his people in Judah by giving them good crops again. With her two daughters-in-law, Ruth and Orpah, she set out on a journey back to Bethlehem. But before they had walked very far, Naomi questioned the wisdom of bringing Moabite women into Israelite territory. Would the young women fit in? Would they find husbands? Would they be willing to worship the God of Israel?

She didn't keep her concerns to herself. "Maybe you should just go back home, to your mothers," she said. "You're young. You want children. I have no more sons for you. There's time for you to find another husband here with your people."

At this juncture, the two daughters-in-law made two different choices. With tears, Orpah kissed Naomi good-bye and returned back to the familiar—her mother's home in Moab. But Ruth wanted to choose a new path. She clung to Naomi, whom she had grown to love. The biblical account says that Naomi felt embittered by her loss. Even so, Ruth must have noticed and been attracted to her good and godly character. Ruth cried out, "Don't ask me to leave you. I will go with you. Your people will be my people, and your God my God."

For Ruth this decision meant abandoning her tribal identity and her religious affiliation. She knew she wanted to follow Naomi and worship the God of Israel. Ruth must have realized that her mother-in-law served the true God, and she decided to follow him wholeheartedly. I see the rest of her wonderful story unfolding from this moment of decision. *God, I follow you. I will put my life in your hands.*

Destitute but hopeful, Ruth and Naomi returned to Israel, where they could take advantage of a law that allowed poor widows to glean from the fields after the harvesters had completed their work. Ruth did not understand how God would work in her life, but she followed God as she accompanied Naomi to Bethlehem. Like a child who trusts her father not to drop her, she jumped into God's arms and trusted him to accomplish her dream of having a husband and children.

The name *Ruth* means *friendship,* and Ruth was certainly a friend to her mother-in-law. Though we don't know how old Naomi was, apparently Ruth felt Naomi should stay home and "tend the hearth," while Ruth went out to provide for them. Every morning Ruth rose and went to the fields to glean enough grain to make bread. The fields belonged to Boaz, a close relative of Naomi's husband.

Our first glimpse of Boaz is significant: He arrives at his fields and greets his workers with a blessing: "The Lord be with you!" (Ruth 2:4). When he noticed the unfamiliar young woman, he asked one of his workers who she was.

"She is the Moabitess who came back from Moab with Naomi. She said, 'Please let me glean and gather among the sheaves behind the harvesters.' She went into the field and has worked steadily from morning till now, except for a short rest in the shelter" (Ruth 2:6–7).

From here on out the story is about Boaz as much as it is about Ruth and Naomi. "Don't go away from here," he tells Ruth. "Stay here with my servant girls. Watch the field where the men are harvesting, and follow along after the girls. I have told the men not to touch you. And whenever you are thirsty, go and get a drink from the water jars the men have filled" (Ruth 2:8–9).

Ruth in turn wonders why he is being so kind to her. And he has a ready reason: He's heard about her commitment to and care of Naomi—and her commitment to God. "May you be richly rewarded by the Lord, the God of Israel, under whose wings you have come to take refuge" (Ruth 2:12).

That noon Boaz gave Ruth some bread for her lunch. And that evening Naomi was impressed with the bundle of barley she brought home. "Where did you get all this?" Naomi asked. "From Boaz? Why, he's a close family member—a kinsman redeemer." A kinsman-redeemer of Naomi's husband was a man who had the first option to purchase any of the deceased man's property and had some responsibility to marry a widow—in this case young Ruth—in order to carry on the family lineage.

Naomi quickly began to advise Ruth on how to make this match. And her plan worked; it involved Ruth saying to Boaz, "Spread the corner of your garment over me, since you are a kinsman-redeemer" (Ruth 3:9). The New International Version Study Bible says this is "a request for marriage" and notes that in this verse the word *corner* is a play on the word *wings* as used earlier when Boaz told Ruth that she had taken refuge under the Lord's wings. The biblical writer wants us to see Boaz's commitment as a type of our spiritual redemption.

How did Boaz respond? He said, "And now, my daughter, don't be afraid. I will do for you all you ask" (Ruth 3:11).

After clearing the matter with an even closer relative, Boaz married Ruth. His compassionate action symbolizes what Christ did for us. Like Ruth, we were born outside the redeemer's family, but he loved us enough to redeem us.

> So Boaz took Ruth and she became his wife. Then he went to her, and the Lord enabled her to conceive, and she gave birth to a son. The women said to Naomi, "Praise be to the Lord, who this day has not left you without a kinsman-redeemer. May he become famous throughout Israel! He will renew your life and sustain you in your old age. For your daughter-in-law, who loves you and who is better to you than seven sons, has given him birth" (Ruth 4:13–15).

The last few verses of the book of Ruth tell us that Ruth's redemption blessed not only her, but generations to come. A short genealogy states that the son born to Ruth and Boaz was the grandfather of King David, the ancestor of my Redeemer—born centuries later in Bethlehem.

A QUEEN'S CONVERSION

Ruth's redemptive story reminds me of the conversion of another woman I have recently discovered. The remarkable

Queen Ka'ahumanu of Hawaii, who was surprised by God during her regent reign, lived early in the nineteenth century. The widow of King Kamehameha, Queen Ka'ahumanu led the islands away from idol worship and paganism, putting a stop to the human sacrifice that had been practiced in Hawaii for centuries. The Spirit of God had been working in the queen's heart, urging her to seek Truth. She discovered it in 1820, when Hiram Bingham and a group of missionaries landed their ship *Thaddeus* on the islands.

After hearing the missionaries' message, Queen Ka'ahumanu made the decision to accept Christ and spread the gospel among the islands. She incorporated three of the Ten Commandments—those against stealing, murder, and adultery—into Hawaiian law. She made certain that children in schools were taught about Christianity.

Years later, as the queen lay upon her deathbed, Bingham presented her with his newly completed Hawaiian translation of the New Testament. She declared it good, then spoke her last words: "I am going where the mansions are ready."[1]

Queen Ka'ahumanu's courageous example and faith gave other Hawaiians courage to leave the old ways. The Christian missionaries also baptized the high chiefess Kapiolani, who guided the people away from superstition and human sacrifice to Pele, the volcano goddess. Emboldened by her newfound faith, Kapiolani descended into the crater of the volcano Kilauea and defied Pele by eating some of the goddess's sacred berries. While her people looked on in amazement, she proclaimed, "Jehovah is my God. He kindled these fires. I fear not Pele. All the gods of Hawaii are vain."[2]

I wonder how many people in Hawaii clung to the old ways of their people like Orpah, who returned to her old land and her old gods? Queen Ka'ahumanu and Kapiolani were like Ruth, who took bold steps to embrace the living God of Israel. Their newfound faith in God set them on a journey that transformed their lives and even the course of world history in ways they didn't understand at the time of their decisions.

For Ruth, turning to the God of Abraham meant leaving her homeland. For Hawaii's great queen, new faith came as she sought Truth and was willing to listen when missionaries arrived at her shore and presented the Gospel. Each woman was delightfully surprised by the Lord's redemptive work in her life. And so was I.

UNDER HIS WINGS

I was in high school when I discovered what it meant to have a personal relationship with Jesus Christ. I had heard about Jesus ever since I was little, but I never understood that I needed to make a decision to ask him to be my Savior. In my efforts to please God and be good, I had joined a youth group at Shades Mountain Baptist Church. One day the Sunday school teacher asked me if I had been baptized. "Yes," I answered, "as a baby in the Episcopal Church."

I thought I had been "saved" all my life. Even though I loved Jesus and had talked about him since childhood, I did not read the Bible or pray consistently until this point when I surrendered my life to him. I had believed that he existed; I had believed in his goodness and love. Finally, I was ready to believe in Jesus enough to trust my life and future to him.

I had been surrounded by good friends while a student in lower grades at the Central Institute for the Deaf, but I felt a lot like Ruth entering a strange country when I enrolled at Berry High School in Birmingham. Although I was somewhat close to one girl who took a sign language class with me, I had very few real friends at Berry. Like Ruth when she first arrived in Bethlehem, I felt lonely. I found myself eating lunch alone, being ignored by classmates who seemed to have known each other since childhood. I tried to read their lips, but since they all talked at the same time, I caught very little of the conversation.

After a while, I gave up and just laughed when the other kids laughed and smiled when they smiled although I didn't have a clue as to what they were talking about. While the other girls chatted about their dates, hobbies, games, clubs, and activities, my mind drifted toward dreams of spotlights and toe shoes.

Sometimes I became angry when I wondered why no one would take the time to talk to me. Didn't they realize I had a brain? I could read lips if someone made the effort to approach me, but they needed to make the first move.

I am so grateful that in this situation I sensed the presence of God, my loving Redeemer—the One whose wings provided refuge for me. I think of the gospel of Luke's account of Jesus comparing himself to a hen who "gathers her chicks under her wings" (13:34). In my difficult teen years of transition, God comforted me in my loneliness, even as he was nudging me to "fear not" and reach beyond my habit of withdrawal.

While I was longing for something to make me acceptable in my peers' eyes, I flipped through an old yearbook and noticed the section for senior superlatives: best dressed, most athletic, most popular, etc. In this section I saw a picture of the Berry High School girls who participated in the annual Junior Miss pageant.

Because I wanted to have something special in the yearbook to show to my children, I decided to enter the Shelby County Junior Miss competition. The pageant program included a choreographed routine. When some of the girls had difficulty with the dance steps, I was more than happy to help them out. I was thrilled to be useful, and I think they were surprised to find out that it was possible—even easy—to communicate with me. I took a lot of time to help them, and they followed my lead in the dance. Their gratitude lifted my self-esteem in ways I had never experienced before. And on the final night of the pageant when the emcee announced that I had won the Spirit Award—a scholarship awarded by the contestants themselves—I felt as happy as if I had been voted homecoming queen of a dozen high schools. Even though I didn't win—I was second runner up and I won the talent competition—the experience brought me out of my isolation and helped me relate to girls my own age.

Like Ruth, I found salvation in a place where I felt like a foreigner. But it was in that place, among people who scarcely knew me, that I sensed God's presence and felt him working in and through my life.

Whether your relationship with Christ the Redeemer is new or long-established, I encourage you to remember a verse from Isaiah that serves as a wonderful metaphor for what redemption is: "Fear not, for I have redeemed you; I have summoned you by name; you are mine" (43:1).

four

SURPRISED BY
ADVERSITY

~

WHEN WE THINK OF ISRAEL'S GREAT WARRIOR KING, WE usually think first of David and his mighty exploits and works—killing Goliath and leading the kingdom of Israel to military victory. Sunday school teachers introduce children to the shepherd boy who was anointed by the prophet Samuel and then went on to become one of the best-known kings in history. David, in fact, is the most famous ancestor of Jesus Christ. Though Jesus was descended from Abraham, Isaac, and Jacob, he is most commonly called the Son of David.

We love to exalt David's triumphs, but this man also suffered through dark times. Though he performed noble deeds, he also committed heinous crimes. Though he yearned for God, he also lusted for carnal pleasures. I doubt there is any character in the Bible who is more fully human—just like you and me.

Though David became king of Israel, he was not born a prince. He was the son of Jesse, a rural settler with eight strong sons, any one of whom appeared to be better "royal" material than David.

The story of the shepherd boy's divine selection begins in the book of 1 Samuel, when the prophet Samuel tells Saul, Israel's first king, that his sons will not inherit the throne: "But now your kingdom will not endure; the Lord has sought out a man after his own heart and appointed him leader of his people, because you have not kept the Lord's command" (13:14).

At this point David was still a boy. A short time later Samuel journeyed to Jesse's home and announced that he had come to anoint one of his sons according to the Lord's command. Astounded and pleased, Jesse summoned his older sons and paraded them before Samuel.

> Jesse had seven of his sons pass before Samuel, but Samuel said to him, "The Lord has not chosen these." So he asked Jesse, "Are these all the sons you have?"
>
> "There is still the youngest," Jesse answered, "but he is tending the sheep."
>
> Samuel said, "Send for him; we will not sit down until he arrives" (1 Sam. 16:10–11).

After his anointing with oil, which symbolically set him apart for the Lord's service, David did not automatically become king. Saul was still alive—and desperately moody. When he sent out scouts to find a musician who could calm his nerves, they tracked down a young skilled harpist: David, the son of Jesse. For a while David "went back and forth from Saul to tend his father's sheep" (1 Sam. 17:15). On one journey to Saul's battlefield camp, the scrappy young David—refusing to put on the king's protective armor—killed the taunting giant Goliath with one well-aimed stone from a slingshot.

ON THE RUN

The people hailed David as a hero, but fame is a two-edged sword. As thousands of people chanted David's name, King Saul grew envious. Though Saul's son Jonathan loved the young shepherd like a brother and Saul's daughter Michal had married David, Saul's hatred of his rival festered until he obsessed over murdering him. Fleeing for his life, David lived like an outlaw in the wilderness caves.

Can you imagine how he felt? The king's envy forced the gifted and sensitive David, who had been blessed by God and anointed by God's prophet, to live on the run while the king's warriors scoured the mountains searching for him.

Twice Saul came close enough that David could have killed him, but David would not raise a hand against Saul. On the second such encounter, in the dead of night when all the king's men were asleep, David crept into Saul's camp and took the spear and water jug by Saul's head. From a safe distance, David called out, waking Saul and taunting his guard, Abner:

> "Why didn't you guard your lord the king? . . .
> Look around you. Where are the king's spear and
> water jug that were near his head?"
>
> Saul recognized David's voice and said, "Is that
> your voice, David my son?"
>
> David replied, "Yes it is, my lord the king." And
> he added, "Why is my lord pursuing his servant?
> What have I done, and what wrong am I guilty of?
> Now let my lord the king listen to his servant's
> words. If the Lord has incited you against me, then
> may he accept an offering. If, however, men have
> done it, may they be cursed before the Lord!"
> (1 Sam. 26:15–19).

I love David's humility. Though Saul had driven him
from his well-deserved position in the king's court, David
refused to harm his enemy, because he knew God had chosen Saul as Israel's first king. Though David knew he was
God's choice for Israel's future, he was not willing to rush
to his promised position.

How many of us would have been so faithful and so
patient? How often do we try to rush into things for which
we may not yet be prepared?

Our society has become accustomed to instant coffee,
microwave meals, and quick access to information via the
Internet. We don't like to wait, but sometimes we learn
while we're waiting. During the time of waiting, God leads
us through the valley and refines our character.

BEYOND COMPLACENCY

In time, Jonathan was killed and Saul was critically
wounded in a battle—not against David, but against the

Philistines. Feeling hopelessly surrounded, Saul fell on his own sword. David was devastated by the news of the deaths of Saul and Jonathan. The last verse in 2 Samuel 1 includes a long eulogy that ends: "How the mighty have fallen!"

After Saul's death David was again anointed king over his own tribe of Judah and later, when he was thirty years old, over all of Israel. Though he accomplished many great things, he soon found himself waiting again. More than anything, David wanted to build a temple in which the children of Israel could worship the Lord. Blessed with great wealth, he had amassed vast quantities of gold, silver, brass, wood, and stone. He told the prophet Nathan, "Here I am, living in a palace of cedar, while the ark of God remains in a tent" (2 Sam. 7:2).

Through Nathan, God assured David that a temple would be built, but not by David. "I will raise up your offspring to succeed you.... He is the one who will build a house for my Name" (7:12–13). Then God made a greater promise: "Your house and your kingdom will endure forever before me" (7:16).

David clung to this bright dream, believing God would prove himself faithful and allow one of his sons to complete the work.

I've learned one important thing through David's life story: No matter how great the dream we accomplish, until God takes us home, we are never finished. God always has another task in the future, another job for us to do—even if it is preparing our children to accomplish the tasks God sets before them. Our role may be something different from what we have done in the past; it may be something the world considers simple, but the task ahead of us is always important.

What if someone had met young David an hour after he killed Goliath and said, "Enjoy the moment, kiddo, because this is the highlight of your life. It's not going to get any better than this"?

I don't know how that would make you feel, but I know my heart would have dropped to my toes. When I received the Miss America crown, it would have been easy to concentrate on the fact that I had come to the end of a long stretch of pageants and challenges. What if some snide little imp had perched on my shoulder and whispered, "Enjoy the moment, Heather, because it's not going to get any better than this. The rest of your life is going to be one downhill slide"?

Do not listen to the niggling voice of cynicism that can whisper in your ear after you have met a goal or won a great victory. The mountaintops in your future may be completely different from those of your past, but you will still experience victories. God will use his servants as long as they are willing to be tools in his hand.

I've had many glorious experiences since winning the Miss America crown. I have married and given birth to two beautiful boys, and nothing in my early life could ever come close to those joyful moments. I know the future will hold many challenges and victories that result from my career, motherhood, and marriage. Those will be quite different from my pageant experiences, and I'll learn new and different lessons along the way. But I look forward to those challenges and victories.

David endured many trials in his times of waiting and his time of ruling—but he remained faithful to God in adversity. Despite his failings, he will forever be known as the man "after God's own heart."

P E R S E V E R A N C E P A Y S

One of my most prized possessions is a book by Helen Keller, the woman who taught the world that blindness and deafness are not insurmountable obstacles. In her autobiography *Midstream, My Later Life,* she wrote about living through adversity. Instead of fretting about not being able to hear or see, Helen concentrated on what she *could* do. She allowed God to use her adversity to demonstrate not only the excellence of the human will, but also his power to overcome hardship.

Though Helen was trapped in a body that could not see, hear, or speak for most of her first six years, she still sensed *something.* She had lived almost like an animal, frustrated to the point of temper tantrums, because the world did not make sense.

Finally, a teacher sent to her family's home in Alabama reached Helen by pumping well water over her hand and then spelling w-a-t-e-r in her palm. Her patient teacher, Anne Sullivan, had done this many times before, but finally the light of understanding dawned. This simple act was the beginning of Helen's communication with the world.

Helen suddenly understood that objects had names, and that someone had been trying to tell her what they were. By the end of that day she had learned thirty words. And in time she realized that the natural world was well ordered and sequenced.

Remarkably, Helen did not grow bitter toward the God who had ordered all things and allowed her to become deaf and blind through a childhood illness. She wrote, "There is still in the lowliest of men and women something called faith, which will respond to those speaking with the greatest of all authority, the authority of an inward conviction of the truth of God's message."[1]

I love Helen Keller because she was devoted to saving people from darkness—not the darkness she suffered from as a blind person, but darkness of the spirit. She wanted people to experience the light God brings to our lives.

Helen's spiritual awakening occurred in a most unusual way. She had been sitting in her room reading a book about Greece when she suddenly realized that life exists on more than physical and emotional planes:

> I had been sitting quietly in the library for half an hour. I turned to my teacher and said, "Such a strange thing has happened! I have been far away all this time, and I haven't left the room."
>
> "What do you mean, Helen?" she asked, surprised.
>
> "Why," I cried, "I have been in Athens!"
>
> Scarcely were the words out of my mouth when a bright, amazing realization seemed to catch my mind and set it ablaze. I perceived the realness of

my soul and its sheer independence of all conditions of place and body. It was clear to me that it was because I was a spirit that I had so vividly "seen" and felt a place thousands of miles away. Space was nothing to spirit! In that new consciousness shone the presence of God, who is a spirit everywhere at once, the Creator dwelling in all the universe simultaneously.

The fact that my small soul could reach out over continents and seas to Greece, despite a blind, deaf, and stumbling body, sent another exulting emotion rushing over me. I had broken through my limitations and found in the sense of touch an eye. I could read the thoughts of wise men and women— thoughts that had for ages survived their mortal life—and could possess them as part of myself.

If this were true, how much more could God, the uncircumscribed spirit, cancel the harms of nature—accident, pain, destruction—and reach out to his children! Deafness and blindness, then, were of no real account. They were to be relegated to the outer circle of my life. Of course I did not sense any such process with my child-mind; but I did know that I, the real I, could leave the library and visit any place I wanted to, mentally, and I was happy. That was the little seed from which grew my interest in spiritual subjects.[2]

Helen's life did not become simple and easy once her teacher helped her make sense of the world. Because Helen was deaf, she didn't speak until Anne Sullivan taught her to talk. Deaf people, of course, have vocal cords, but it is hard to modulate a voice when you cannot hear the voices of other people. I know, because I have this problem too. I can read lips and talk on the telephone (with the help of my hearing aid), but the ending sounds of words often escape me. A lifetime of hard, patient work and pageant experiences have helped me to be confident when I stand to speak before crowds, but sometimes I still worry.

I can relate to Helen's frustration as she stood before a large crowd to make her first speech.

> Oh, that first appearance in Montclair, New Jersey! Until my dying day I shall think of that stage as a pillory where I stood cold, riveted, trembling, voiceless. Words thronged to my lips, but no syllable could I utter. At last I forced a sound. It felt to me like a cannon going off, but they told me afterwards it was a mere whisper.... Everyone was kind and sympathetic, but I knew I had failed. All the eloquence which was to bring light to the blind lay crumpled at my feet. I came off the stage in despair, my face deluged with tears, my breast heaving with sobs, my whole body crying out, "Oh, it is too difficult, too difficult, I cannot do the impossible." But in a little while faith and hope and love came back and I returned to my practicing.[3]

Helen did not give up. She went on to become one of the most beloved speakers and authors of the twentieth century. I will not give up either, and neither should you— no matter what task and goal God has called you to carry out. Whether you are struggling to get an education, raise your children, excel in your job, or provide for your family, do not let the giants of the world intimidate you into defeat.

Like Helen Keller, the songwriter Fanny Crosby lost her sight in infancy. Yet she was able to write:

> Not to the strong is the battle,
> Not to the swift is the race,
> But to the true and the faithful
> Victory is promised through grace.

As a child Crosby learned to read Braille, but she found it difficult because her fingers were callused from playing the harp and guitar. As the years passed, she became acquainted with pain and hardship—her only child died in infancy, a loss she was never able to discuss. Fanny died in 1915 at the age of ninety-five, and she's still remembered for writing the words to more than eight thousand gospel songs including "Blessed Assurance." Despite adversity and pain, she could say,

> Perfect submission, all is at rest,
> I in my Savior am happy and blest;
> Watching and waiting, looking above,
> Filled with his goodness, lost in his love.

Crosby understood what David learned about the rewards of patience. Fulfillment and joy are not found in being the biggest soldier or the fastest runner. They are found in being true and faithful, persistent and patient, and then depending on God's great grace even in the midst of adversity.

five

SURPRISED BY DELIVERANCE

THE FIERY TRIAL

The book of Daniel begins with an account of how Nebuchadnezzar, king of Babylon, surrounded Jerusalem with his army. Scripture says that the Lord delivered the king of Judah into the foreign king's hand, along with some of the golden articles from the Temple. These Nebuchadnezzar carried off to Babylon and displayed in the treasure house of his false god.

Nebuchadnezzar didn't only take treasures—he also took men, women, and children to work in his royal city as slaves. And once the horde reached Babylon, the chief of the king's court officials sorted through the captives, like a farmer culling weak cattle from strong. He dispatched the weak and elderly to perform menial labor and sent brawny men to the quarries.

But Nebuchadnezzar wasn't solely interested in brute strength, he also appreciated brains. He ordered Ashpenaz, chief of his court, to bring in some of the Israelites from the royal family and the nobility—young men without any physical defect, handsome, showing aptitude for every kind of learning, well informed, quick to understand, and qualified to serve in the king's palace. The king then commanded Ashpenaz to teach these young men the language and literature of the Babylonians.

Because of their stellar qualities, these chosen few were given the best Babylon could offer—food and wine from the king's table and the finest instructors in Babylon. After three years of palace training, Nebuchadnezzar expected them to go to work—for *him*.

These young men, wrenched from their homes and families, faced a bitter reality. The king of Judah had been soundly vanquished, and there was no Marine Corps to come dashing in for a last-minute rescue; they were not going home in the near future, if at all. If they prayed for deliverance, those prayers were answered with a resounding no. God clearly had a purpose for these men in a foreign land.

Among the youths selected for royal service, four from the tribe of Judah were given new Babylonian names. Daniel became Belteshazzar; Hananiah became Shadrach; Mishael became Meshach; and Azariah became Abednego. I can almost see them standing before central processing desks like those at Ellis Island where immigrants entered the United States and received American-sounding surnames.

Reading the biblical account of these young men, some-thing struck me: Though they were captives, they were not defeated. These four did not stumble through the palace doors with downcast eyes and tear-stained cheeks. They went with a firm belief in the sovereignty of their God and with convic-tions regarding their personal holiness. Though forced to live in a pagan king's palace, they decided they would not become a compliant part of the landscape. They would be *in* the palace, perhaps, but they would not be *of* it.

These four foreigners caused a stir almost immediately. As soon as they entered the palace, where they were told about their "special" diet, Daniel lifted his hand. "We are not unaware of the honor you are attempting to give us," he said, speaking for the quartet. "But we will not eat food from the king's table."

Hold everything! The king's captain must have dropped his jaw and gaped at Daniel. Not eat from the king's table? Why, certain ambitious men in Babylon would give their eldest daughters for a chance to enjoy delicacies from the king's chef! But Daniel remained firm in his resolve. We don't know exactly why he and the others felt so strongly about refusing the king's food. It's unlikely they were vege-tarians, because the Israelites freely ate meat; but it's entirely possible the food came from offerings to the king's false god. As a servant of the true God, Daniel wanted nothing to do with idolatry.

Scripture says that "God had caused the official to show favor and sympathy to Daniel," but, even so, the man told Daniel, "I am afraid of my lord the king, who has

assigned your food and drink. Why should he see you looking worse than the other young men your age? The king
would then have my head because of you" (Dan. 1:10).

Daniel quickly proposed an alternate menu for the four
young men.

> Please test your servants for ten days: Give us noth-
> ing but vegetables to eat and water to drink. Then
> compare our appearance with that of the young
> men who eat the royal food, and treat your servants
> in accordance with what you see (Dan. 1:12–13).

What was the result?

> At the end of the ten days they looked healthier
> and better nourished than any of the young men
> who ate the royal food. So the guard took away
> their choice food and the wine they were to drink
> and gave them vegetables instead (Dan.1:15–16).

The "Daniel diet" was a rousing success! And Daniel's
example of firm resolve only increased the Babylonians'
respect for him.

In time, Daniel and his friends became trusted officials.
And after Daniel interpreted a troublesome dream for the
king, he elevated all four young men. He made Shadrach,
Meshach, and Abednego province administrators and kept
Daniel at the royal court.

All was proceeding peacefully for the Hebrews until the
king's ego intervened. God prepared to surprise not only
the captives, but the entire kingdom!

Nebuchadnezzar made and set on display a huge golden
image, ninety feet high and nine feet wide. He summoned all

governmental officials from across the country to the dedi-
cation ceremony.

> Then the herald loudly proclaimed, "This is what
> you are commanded to do. . . . As soon as you hear
> the . . . music, you must fall down and worship the
> image of gold that King Nebuchadnezzar has set
> up. Whoever does not fall down and worship will
> immediately be thrown into a blazing furnace"
> (Dan. 3:4–7).

Can you imagine this scene? The king creates a nine-
story statue to represent himself, puts it out in the center
of an open plain, and assembles his house band at its base.
Whenever the band begins to play (probably any time they
catch a glimpse of the king in the vicinity), anyone passing
by has to immediately drop to his knees and kneel in the
dust before the statue.

I think Daniel, Shadrach, Meshach, and Abednego
quietly decide they would stay away from the king statue
and his band. They weren't out to make trouble; they only
wanted to do the job God had given them to do.

But you can't avoid trouble when it comes looking
for you. Some of the king's men went straight to the king
when they noticed that the young Hebrews weren't
complying with the command like everyone else. " 'There
are some Jews whom you have set over the affairs of the
province of Babylon—Shadrach, Meshach and Abednego—
who pay no attention to you, O king. They neither serve
your gods nor worship the image of gold you have set
up' " (Dan. 3:12).

It's not clear where Daniel is at this point, but the biblical account focuses in on his three friends. Nebuchadnezzar fumed when he heard they were not obeying his edict. He called them in and personally demanded that they bow before his golden idol. But he forgot that those men did not fear his threats, as they served a much greater authority.

> Shadrach, Meshach and Abednego replied to the king, "O Nebuchadnezzar, we do not need to defend ourselves before you in this matter. If we are thrown into the blazing furnace, the God we serve is able to save us from it, and he will rescue us from your hand, O king. But even if he does not, we want you to know, O king, that we will not serve your gods or worship the image of gold you have set up" (Dan. 3:16–18).

Shadrach, Meshach, and Abednego had no guarantees that God would deliver them. After all, he hadn't delivered them from captivity, but had instead used them to bring honor and glory to his name in Babylon. Even knowing that God might choose to glorify himself through death instead of deliverance, they did not waver in their commitment to Truth. They did not try to beg, make a deal, or avoid the issue. They stood firm upon their faith in the one true God, and refused to bow to a pagan idol.

Nebuchadnezzar wasn't just angry—he was flaming with rage! He had the furnace heated higher than it had ever been, seven times hotter than it should be. Though his four prisoners did not protest, he called for the strongest men in his army to bind the stubborn captives. Then he lost his army's strongest warriors as the superheated fire devoured the oxygen in the area, instantly killing those who had escorted the captives to the fiery furnace.

But even in the middle of the blazing furnace, Shadrach, Meshach, and Abednego remained unharmed. Only the ropes that bound their arms burned. They did not faint from breathing the superheated air, they did not fall, and they did not find themselves alone.

> Then King Nebuchadnezzar leaped to his feet in amazement and asked his advisers, "Weren't there three men that we tied up and threw into the fire?"
> They replied, "Certainly, O king."
> He said, "Look! I see four men walking around in the fire, unbound and unharmed, and the fourth looks like a son of the gods" (Dan. 3:24–25).

God did not abandon his three servants. In the midst of their trial, he sent either an angel or his son to stand with them. That heavenly visitor walked among the flames with them, imparting strength and courage. His appearance was so startling, so impressive, that the king recognized the fourth man for who he was.

How quickly the king changed his attitude! Nebuchadnezzar approached the opening of the blazing furnace and lifted his voice in a most royal shout: "Shadrach, Meshach and Abednego, servants of the Most High God, come out!"

So Shadrach, Meshach, and Abednego walked out of the fire, and all the king's men crowded around them. They saw that the fire had not harmed the Hebrews' bodies, nor was a hair of their heads singed, nor were their robes scorched. Those young men looked like they had just come from a restful day at the beach, and they didn't even smell of smoke!

At that moment, Nebuchadnezzar realized that he had met servants of a mightier king than himself. Bowing in submission, he said,

> "Praise be to the God of Shadrach, Meshach and Abednego, who has sent his angel and rescued his servants! They trusted in him and defied the king's command and were willing to give up their lives rather than serve or worship any god except their own God" (Dan. 3:28).

Because of this witness of God's power, Nebuchadnezzar himself turned to the God of Israel and promoted Shadrach, Meshach, and Abednego to even better positions. Those young men still didn't get to go home, but God had a plan for them even in the land of their captivity.

God did a mighty work that day. He took three believers with firm faith and worked a miracle that changed a kingdom, turning idol worshippers to God worshippers! There is only one God worthy of worship. And he is powerful and willing to surprise his people with unexpected deliverance.

DELIVERED FOR A PURPOSE

God delivered me from death when I was only eighteen months old. As I mentioned earlier, a mysterious infection sent my fever soaring above 104 degrees. What seemed to have been a routine illness became a life-or-death situation.

My parents prayed, the doctors tried strong antibiotics, and my life was spared. I praise God for the antibiotics that spared my life, and yet I know that as a result came the mixed blessing of deafness.

I call deafness a mixed blessing because the loss of my hearing changed my life completely. I would not be who I am if I had kept my hearing. Though I may have loved dancing, I might not have retreated to the peace of the dance studio if I had grown up as a hearing child. The studio was my refuge, the place where my thoughts could soar, and I could forget about the frustrations of learning to communicate.

Do you see how God works?

A friend of mine told me that the other day she and her husband were grumbling about how hard it was to raise teenagers. "My kids are seventeen and eighteen," she said, "and they're driving us crazy! Last week my husband and I looked at each other, and I said, 'Tell me again why we wanted to have kids.'

"He grinned and said, 'Because we need them. If we didn't have kids, we'd be rich, spoiled, and shallow. Worst of all, we wouldn't be able to sympathize with other struggling parents.'"

How true! Sometimes our blessings teach us through the trials they bring. Sometimes God delivers us out of all our trials. Sometimes he keeps us in trials so someone else can be delivered.

CALLED TO DELIVER OTHERS

A few days ago I read a moving newspaper article about a family that adopted eight children from an orphanage in

Russia. With two biological children already, the adoption expanded their family to twelve—and they lived in a three-bedroom ranch house. I couldn't understand why they would take in so many children.

But as I kept reading, I realized that they did not set out to adopt eight children. Their mission of mercy—to deliver these children from distressing circumstances and give them a home—unfolded over time, as God showed them the need. Adopting children wasn't part of their plan at all until after the tragic car-accident death of their biological son, only a day shy of his tenth birthday. The idea was planted by their daughter who later commented, "Our family would never be right with just two children." In time the parents went to Russia and brought home a sibling pair, a brother and a sister.

During the first year, their newly adopted daughter cried herself to sleep every night because she missed her best friend, a girl still at the Russian orphanage. She explained that the two of them had always held hands at night until they fell asleep. Having mercy on this heartbroken child, the mother went back to Russia to find the best friend. Once there, she discovered that the girl had two brothers. She did not have the heart to separate a sibling group, so she brought all three children home.

In the meantime, their first adopted son announced that he had been praying that his new family would adopt his other three sisters, who still lived with their biological parents. The American mother tried to explain that this was impossible; they couldn't go to Russia and "take" the three girls. But that didn't keep the boy from praying.

And his prayer was answered. Can you imagine how surprised this American family was to receive news from Russia? The three sisters were suddenly available for adoption, abandoned by their mother after their father had been killed in a fire. Once again, the American mother packed her bags and boarded a jet plane. When she arrived in Russia, one of the three sisters recognized her from a photo at the children's home. "I always dreamed I would meet you," she said.

These missions of mercy may or may not have saved the children's lives, but they illustrate how God frequently works to deliver people in distress as we make ourselves available to be agents of deliverance.[1]

LINCOLN'S LEGACY

Abraham Lincoln, our nation's greatest president, was blessed and burdened with leading our country during its darkest hour. A deeply spiritual man, he understood the importance of standing up—even fighting—for what is right. He also understood the importance of mercy in being the agent of deliverance for others.

Once Lincoln's young son Tad, who was playing with dolls—probably yesteryear's version of GI Joe—found his doll named Jack guilty of insubordination and then sentenced him to death. Hearing about this, Lincoln wrote Tad a note: "The doll Jack is pardoned. By order of the President." He officially signed the paper "A. Lincoln."[2]

Lincoln, who wielded great authority, wanted his son to grow up knowing the importance and power of mercy.

On another occasion the president noticed a frail drummer boy and called him out of the crowd.

> "Come here, my boy, and tell me what you want."
> The boy . . . said, "Mr. President, I have been a drummer in a regiment for two years, and my colonel got angry with me and turned me off; I was taken sick, and have been a long time in a hospital. This is the first time I have been out, and I came to see if you could not do something for me."
>
> The President . . . asked him where he lived. "I have no home," answered the boy. "Where is your father?" "He died in the army," was the reply. "Where is your mother?" continued the President. "My mother is dead also. I have no mother, no father, no brothers, no sisters, and"—bursting into tears—"no friends. Nobody cares for me."
>
> Mr. Lincoln's eyes filled with tears, and he said to him, "Can't you sell newspapers?" "No," said the boy. "I am too weak, and the surgeon of the hospital told me I must leave, and I have no place to go." . . . The President drew forth a card, addressed it to certain officials to whom his request was law, and gave special directions to "care for this poor boy."[3]

On October 6, 1862, President Lincoln indirectly compared the Civil War to the test Shadrach, Meshach, and Abednego had endured. Confiding in four Quaker guests, he said,

> We are indeed going through a great trial—a fiery trial. In the very responsible position in which I happen to be placed, being a humble instrument in

the hands of our Heavenly Father, as I am, and as we all are, to work out His great purposes, I have desired that all my works and acts may be according to His will, and that it might be so, I have sought His aid.[4]

Lincoln did not face a fiery furnace, but he faced the fires of war. Personally, I think he would have rather taken a walk through Nebuchadnezzar's fireplace with the angel of the Lord than face the bloody struggle that divided our nation.

God answered Lincoln's prayers for the nation, but not as Lincoln might have wished. More than two years later, a month before the end of the War, in his Second Inaugural Address, Lincoln publicly admitted:

> Neither party expected for the war the magnitude or the duration which it has already attained. . . . Both [North and South] read the same Bible and pray to the same God, and each invokes His aid against the other.

Referring to slavery, he continued,

> It may seem strange that any man should dare ask a just God's assistance in wringing their bread from the sweat of other men's faces, but let us judge not, that we be not judged.
>
> The prayers of both could not be answered. That of neither has been answered fully. The Almighty has his own purposes.[5]

By the time the War ended, a million men were dead or wounded; such casualties were hardly a satisfying answer to either side's prayer. Though in his Second Inaugural speech he asked for "malice toward none" and "charity for all," he was assassinated a week after Lee's surrender. Lincoln was not personally delivered from his trial, but as he placed the good of the nation over self-preservation, God used him to deliver thousands of other Americans.

"Wait a minute," you may be saying. "Lincoln may have delivered others, but God didn't deliver Lincoln from the assassin! Every day people die unexpectedly; God doesn't deliver them from death."

But in the larger, spiritual realm, God delivers us even if he chooses to take our souls to heaven.

The night he was killed at Ford's Theater, President Lincoln told his wife, Mary, about an unfulfilled dream. She later recalled his final words: that he hoped to be able to visit the city of Jerusalem, where Jesus had walked.

Minutes later Lincoln drew his last breath. Mrs. Lincoln realized the significance of his comment, noting that the "good President was carried by angels to the New Jerusalem above."[6]

As Lincoln himself said, "Surely God would not have created such a being as man, with an ability to grasp the infinite, to exist only for a day. No, no, man was made for immortality."[7]

As the years pass, I am confident that God will deliver me as he chooses. I love the promise found in Isaiah 46:4:

> Even to your old age and gray hairs I am he,
> I am he who will sustain you.
> I have made you and I will carry you;
> I will sustain you and I will rescue you.

No matter what trials come your way today, God is able to rescue you. Trust him, and let him surprise you with his deliverance!

> When you pass through the waters,
> I will be with you. . . .
> When you walk through the fire,
> you will not be burned;
> the flames will not set you ablaze.
> For I am the Lord your God (Isa. 43:2–3).

SURPRISED
BY LOVE

〜

HOSEA'S DEDICATION

One of the most touching and unusual love stories of all time is found in the Old Testament. The prophet Hosea, the son of Beeri, lived more than seven hundred years before Christ. Through his life and ministry God revealed his unconditional love for his people. This love was represented by Hosea's commitment to his wife.

"What's so unusual about that?" you may be asking. "Husbands are supposed to love their wives."

Yes, they are. And Hosea loved his wife, Gomer, but she did not return that love easily. For Gomer, you see, was a prostitute. At the beginning of the book that bears Hosea's name, God told him to "'Go, take to yourself an adulterous wife'" (1:2). God kept talking, giving Hosea a reason for this command: "'because the land is guilty of the vilest adultery in departing from the Lord.' So he married Gomer daughter of Diblaim, and she conceived and bore him a son" (1:2–3).

I am sure Hosea dreamed of having a beautiful family and a faithful wife who would never abandon him and his children. He was a good man, one who heard and obeyed the voice of the Lord. If ever a man deserved a faithful and loving wife, Hosea did.

At first, things seemed to go well for the new family. Gomer gave birth to three children, a daughter and two sons. The names of the two younger babies, meaning "not pitied" and "not of my people," imply that Hosea believed they were not his offspring. Then, sometime after weaning her third child, Gomer left Hosea and went to live with another man.

Hosea not only had to live with the heartache of losing his wife, but he also had to care for three young children who were probably not his! Any other man, particularly one of that time, might have been tempted to forget about his unfaithful wife and abandon the children. But the voice of the Lord came to Hosea again:

> The Lord said to me, "Go, show your love to your wife again, though she is loved by another and is an adulteress. Love her as the Lord loves the Israelites, though they turn to other gods and love the sacred raisin cakes."
>
> So I bought her for fifteen shekels of silver and about a homer and a lethek of barley. Then I told

her, "You are to live with me many days; you must
not be a prostitute or be intimate with any man,
and I will live with you" (Hosea 3:1–3).

Hosea didn't just say, "Come home, Gomer." He had
to buy her from another man; he had to redeem her at great
personal cost. She was his wife, he loved her, and he was
willing to pay the price her illegitimate lover demanded.

I don't know how Hosea managed to forgive his unfaithful wife. I don't know if I could have done what he did. At
this point, when God tells Hosea to bring his wife back
home, the book of Hosea turns to the relationship between
God and Israel. Hosea paints a picture of what God did for
his people and what Jesus did for everyone. God loves us, and
though most of us would like to love God, we are distracted
by our own sinful desires and our lust for pleasure. We
become unfaithful to him, yet God was willing to redeem us.
Jesus paid the price for our redemption with his own life.
Earthly marriage is a symbol of the love that exists between
God and people, in particular, between Christ and his
Church.

In Hosea's prophetic book, Gomer isn't mentioned
again. But I'm sure of one thing: Gomer was amazed by the
depth of Hosea's love for her.

MEETING AND MAKING MY MATCH

Many people find that marriage brings a taste of heaven
on earth. The love that results in marriage usually involves a
moment of realizing that you are incomplete without another.

I remember the first time I saw the man I would one day marry. In 1995, as Miss America, I went to Washington, D.C. My schedule included a stop at the Capitol, including a visit to the office of the Speaker of the House of Representatives, Newt Gingrich. John McCallum, a young man from Gingrich's home district in Georgia, was one of many people I met that day, but I could not help but be impressed by him. He was tall, dark, and handsome, plus he had a gentle manner and a ready smile—the thing I most remember is his youthful face. I couldn't believe he was old enough to be working in a congressional office!

When Newt was finally able to see me, my traveling companion and I had a picture taken with him, thanked him for his support for the President's Committee on Employment of People with Disabilities, and left.

Not long afterward, I received a letter from John. It being on Congressional letterhead, the Miss America office quickly sent me the letter. Like everyone else, John asked for an autographed picture, then he added, "If you are ever in Washington or the surrounding area, I would be honored to escort you to dinner. God knows there must be times when you want to get away from always being Miss America. I'm sure that can be stressful. I'm a fine and honorable Christian man, and it would be a pleasure to give you the VIP tour of Washington, D.C. I hope you are not offended by my request. If so, please accept my apology."

My traveling companion was more excited about the letter than I was. I didn't have time to date. "Besides," I told her, "I remember him. He's too young."

"Come on . . ." she coaxed—until I said she'd have to call his office and leave a message on his answering machine. With her persistence, (months later) John and I had our first date, which started at a romantic rooftop restaurant overlooking the back lawn of the White House. After John bowed his head and said grace, I let him have it with both barrels: "Tell me how you became a Christian."

"Well, okay . . ." And he then gave me the long version of the circumstances of his asking Jesus Christ to be his Savior. If he had told me that he went to church regularly or gave faithfully to the Red Cross, I would have yawned and gone back to the hotel, pleading a headache. I didn't have time to spend on meaningless relationships. But since John gave me such an honest and sincere answer, I stayed.

After the first course, we went to another nice restaurant for dinner. But near the end of the meal, John excused himself and disappeared for such a long time that I wondered what could have happened. Had I embarrassed him so badly that he'd deserted me? Had my bold question about his faith scared him? Or was he off in a corner somewhere, collecting on a bet he'd made with his buddies— getting a date with me? By the time John finally returned to the table, I was politely furious.

"What took you so long?"

He smiled as he brushed my question aside. "Don't worry."

Had he been in the restroom? Was he sick? He didn't say, and I didn't push. Back at the hotel, he asked if he could take me out again. "Is that okay with you?"

I was surprised by my quick answer—"Sure!"—because I certainly wasn't feeling inclined to give him another opportunity to abandon me in a restaurant. And yet there was something about him . . .

Back in my room, I chatted a few minutes with my traveling companion, when I saw that someone had slipped a note under the door. It was from John:

> Dear Heather:
>   I knew I was going to have a wonderful evening so I took some time to write this short note.
>   First, let me say thanks for calling me back. It's every little boy's dream to meet Miss America. Also, thank you for your kind letter and the autographed picture. It's funny, I think I knew you were a Christian before I met you. You have set such a wonderful example for all Americans who have faced adversity in their lives, and you have proven that a disability can be a blessing in disguise. You have truly proven that the Lord works in mysterious ways.
>   Thanks for such a wonderful evening. I hope you will keep in touch.
>   Sincerely,
>   John McCallum

The second half of the note was written in a different color ink. A few days later when I spoke to John on the phone, I asked why he had taken so long in the restroom.

He laughed. "I wasn't in the restroom. I was sitting at another table, trying to finish that note for you."

And so began our surprising friendship. Maintaining a relationship during those months I was traveling was hectic, but John and I managed to stay in touch. We knew something special was happening between us, and so we followed our hearts and gradually fell in love.

As my Miss America year drew to a close, I dated John as often as I could, which wasn't very often. We weren't "going steady," in fact, I had asked John how he felt about my dating other men as well. To my surprise, he answered, "I don't have time to worry. If you want to date other men, that's between you and God. I trust God completely, and I trust you. If we are meant to become serious, God will show us when the time is right."

I wasn't ready for a serious commitment. I had been so influenced by the "get your education, establish a career" mind-set that I couldn't really see myself getting married before I was twenty-seven or twenty-eight. Most people today wait until they're older to marry, but they feel free to live together. I was committed to chastity, so I knew a live-in relationship wasn't an option for me. But my family and friends continued to urge me to graduate from college and accomplish that dream before marriage.

Still, when you begin to love someone . . .

In November, just two months after I surrendered my Miss America title, John and I were together again in Washington, D.C. I had flown up to work with a speakers' bureau, and John picked me up at my hotel. Before we went to dinner, John suggested that we swing by Newt Gingrich's office so he could pick up some "homework."

I laughed. "I didn't know you had homework." I went with him to Newt's office, then followed him to the balcony of the Capitol, with a view of the Washington Monument and a big, bright moon.

Suddenly suspicious I teased him, "John, you lied to me." We had first met in this building.

"Come over here and sit down." He pointed to a bench. We sat awhile, carrying on an inane and pointless conversation until I stood up and told him I was hungry.

"No, sit down." He practically pulled me down next to him. He seemed overwhelmed, nervous, and more than a little stressed, but he still didn't say anything out of the ordinary.

"John, I'm not kidding, I'm really hungry," I stood again. We walked toward the door into the building, when he grabbed my arm and suddenly fell to one knee. I would have understood his next words even without reading his lips.

"Heather," he said, "I love you with all my heart, all my mind, and all my soul. I want to spend the rest of my life with you. Will you marry me?"

"Yes." I was too excited to cry.

John pulled a ring from his pocket and gently slid it onto my finger.

I felt called to marry John because I loved him, and I also was sure we could serve God more fully as a couple than as two single people. There are times when one plus one adds up to more than two.

I cannot give you advice about who or when you should marry, but I can say this with full authority: God will guide you if you ask him to help you make this most important decision.

God does not usually write our answers in the sky, nor does he speak through horoscopes, Oujia boards, or tarot cards. Sometimes he communicates in a subtle, almost indiscernible inner voice.

Sometimes, particularly when we are young and immature, God speaks through our parents, for as children, we are to obey them.

Sometimes God speaks through his Word. You can be reading the Bible and praying for his voice, and suddenly a verse seems to leap off the page and into your heart. I have heard God speak to me that way.

At other times, God speaks through our spiritual authorities, our pastors and teachers. You can be in church listening to a sermon or watching a minister on television. Suddenly, it is as if the speaker looks you straight in the eye, and he says something that so resonates in your heart that you know you are hearing the words of God.

Sometimes God speaks in a still, small voice that fills your head and heart. If you have been seeking him, when you hear it, you know whose voice it is.

Waiting for his voice can be frustrating at times, especially when your heart wants to race ahead of your head. When you're in love, your heart is full and your body aches for the company of your loved one. We are human, exactly as God created us to be.

But I can assure you that the Lord honors our attempt to seek him in this decision. He will demonstrate his appreciation and his approval of your trust and faith. And you will be glad you sought him. For his guidance is sovereign, even if it does not match the advice given by your aunt, your teacher, or your best friend.

After praying for many weeks and weighing all the options, John and I decided to be married on June 8, 1996. We were excited about the new direction and different path God would lead us down—together.

God told Hosea to marry Gomer—and he led me to John McCallum.

TWO HEADS ARE BETTER THAN ONE

One of the most surprising marriages of human history has to be the marriage between theologian Martin Luther and Katherine von Bora. First, let me give you a little history.

You have probably heard of Martin Luther, the man who effectively began the Great Reformation in 1517. Born in 1483 on the edge of a German forest, Luther entered a monastery when he was young and began to teach the Word of God. As he taught, he found himself surprised by what the Word actually said. Salvation and righteousness do not come by any religious acts we perform, he learned, but they are free gifts from God, attributed to us through faith.

Four years after nailing his Ninety-five Theses to the door of the Wittenberg monastery, Luther stood before the Diet of Worms where two hundred political and religious delegates had gathered. Though he knew his life was at stake, he refused to recant his beliefs, claiming that his authority was the Bible itself. "Here I stand," he told them. "I can do no other. God help me."[1]

A few days later, the Diet of Worms condemned Luther and called for the citizenry's help in arresting him—or killing him on sight. But Luther had already escaped. Leaving the life of a monk, he sought refuge in Saxony, where he found refuge and protection.

Meanwhile, Katherine von Bora, sixteen years younger than Luther, had been living in a convent since her parents deposited her there at the age of nine or ten. She and several of the other nuns heard rumors about the man preaching that salvation was the free gift of God. Hoping to escape the convent, they wrote Luther, asking for help. He arranged for a man named Leonard Kopp to smuggle the nuns to freedom in empty barrels.

Once the nine nuns were safely liberated, Luther had to find jobs or husbands for them. He was successful with eight—but the last one, Katherine, proved to have a sharp tongue and, at twenty-six, she was considered "past her prime."

Luther himself ended up marrying Katherine. At forty-one, he had no burning desire to marry, nor was he passionately in love with his bride. "I am not madly in love, but I cherish her," he said.[2]

In his book *25 Surprising Marriages,* William Petersen recounts that the first year of marriage meant tremendous adjustments for both the runaway nun and the former monk. "There's a lot to get used to in the first year of marriage," Luther admitted. "One wakes up in the morning and finds a pair of pigtails on the pillow which were not there before."[3]

"Before I married," he added, "no one had made up my bed for a whole year. The straw was rotting from my sweat. I wore myself out with work during the day, so that I fell into bed oblivious of everything."[4]

Luther's non-domestic lifestyle changed when Katherine —Katie—entered the home. With a firm hand she took control of Luther's household, his finances, and the six children that followed. Luther, who had said that "God divided the hand into fingers so that money would slip through," suddenly found himself on a budget—and accountable to his wife. Katie was not above hiding money from her husband in order to keep him from giving it away.

The scholastic Luther had to adjust to being knit into the fabric of family life. Accustomed to solitude, he once locked himself in his study for three days until Katie had the door removed. He was studious, she was outspoken; he was generous, she was thrifty. He cared little for the house; the house and garden were the center of her universe.

Despite their differences, the two melded together and became of one mind and one purpose. Luther said,

> To get a wife is easy enough, but to love her with constancy is difficult ... for the mere union of the flesh is not sufficient; there must be congeniality of tastes and character. And that congeniality does not come overnight.
>
> Some marriages were motivated by mere lust, but mere lust is felt even by fleas and lice. Love begins when we wish to serve others ... Of course the Christian should love his wife. He is supposed to love his neighbor, and since his wife is his nearest

neighbor, she should be his deepest love. And she should also be his dearest friend.[5]

Martin Luther not only changed the direction of church history, but in their day he and his Katie changed the common perception of Christian marriage. Luther loved to quote this saying: "Let the wife make her husband glad to come home and let him make her sorry to see him leave."[6]

That's a delightful picture of what marriage should be.

MY PLACE AT HIS SIDE

Marriage has held many surprises. Marriage brought about huge changes in my lifestyle and my future. As a wife, I feel God has called me to be John's helper, and John feels that God has called him into a life of public service in the political realm. This means he must be elected to office, and that means my husband, I, and my children must be subjected to the scrutiny of the press and the voters. I love our country and I love my husband, but there are times when I'd like to throw a baby blanket over my head and run away from politics altogether.

During John's 2000 campaign for Georgia secretary of state, we traveled tens of thousands of miles, zigzagging across the state shaking hands and hearing people's concerns about everything from taxes to school books. The campaign was a mixed experience for me. It is hard to hear opponents mislead the crowd about themselves and distort your husband's positions. We worked hard to reach the Christians we met along the way, for we thought it was important for them to know that John shared their values and wanted to work for them. I volunteered to give speeches at several churches we visited, because I felt God had called me to help John meet this dream God had planted in his spirit.

After a few months, I began to resent the campaign. Campaign workers filled my house. I couldn't use the telephone whenever I wanted to talk to someone in private. I couldn't use the downstairs office because campaign workers had set up to work there. One day I slumped on the sofa and did not want to get up, but I knew "giving up" was no solution. For a while I withdrew—I bought a notebook computer and converted an upstairs bedroom into a place where I could be alone to think.

Then I felt the Lord nudge me back into the role he wanted me to fill. God wanted me to be my husband's companion. He confirmed this one night when John came home and remarked that he had given a terrible speech. I knew he always felt good about his speeches when I stood by his side—something about my being there helped boost his confidence.

It's not easy to be a helper in the political world; politics isn't pretty. But John feels strongly that God has called him to be salt and light in that arena, and I feel strongly that God made me to be my husband's helper.

John didn't win that election, but I'm confident there will be others. And if and when he runs again, I'll be beside him, doing what I can to help.

COMMITMENT COUNTS

Day in and day out, marriage isn't a matter of *feeling*— for most of us, the feelings come first, but strength of will is what makes a marriage last. Emotions are fickle, they come and go like the tides, but a vow to love "for better or worse" is what holds a marriage together.

I'm learning to love when I'm tired—and when I'd rather be doing something else. My husband is learning to love me when I'm not at my best, either.

I have to keep reminding myself that men and women are incompatible by nature. No woman marries someone who is just like herself. Why would anyone want to? If we were both just alike, one of us would be unnecessary. Men and women are different for a reason, and God expects us to honor our commitment and respect our differences.

During our first year of marriage, John and I were arguing one day. I felt a flutter of panic. When John and I were first dating, I never dreamed we would argue. We were in love! Then I realized it is normal for men and women to disagree. The important thing is that we learn to express our disagreements in ways that will not damage our relationship.

I like to putter around in the yard, and John is always reminding me that marriage is like a garden. A good gardener doesn't just set a bunch of plants in the ground and expect them to take care of themselves. You have to work a little every day. You have to keep the weeds pulled and make sure the plants get plenty of sun and water. Sometimes you have to plant; sometimes you have to prune.

How do I relate this to marriage? To have a healthy marriage, I have to keep pulling up my negative thoughts (weeds) and feeding my positive attitudes (flowers). I have to be kind and thoughtful. I have to prune away destructive habits and plant healthy ones. John, of course, will do the same thing to tend his side of our marriage garden. A happy marriage doesn't just happen; it requires patient and loving tending.

Now that we have been married nearly seven years, I've realized that just as God intended Hosea and Gomer's marriage to be a picture of his love for his people, my relationship with John should be an example of a Christian marriage. I don't know what tomorrow holds, but I know I have the opportunity to link my efforts with my husband's. I trust God to lead John, and I trust John to lead our family.

I want to follow God's family design as described in the Bible:

> Wives, submit to your husbands as to the Lord. For the husband is the head of the wife as Christ is the head of the church, his body, of which he is the Savior. Now as the church submits to Christ, so also wives should submit to their husbands in everything.
>
> Husbands, love your wives, just as Christ loved the church and gave himself up for her to make her holy, cleansing her by the washing with water through the word, and to present her to himself as a radiant church, without stain or wrinkle or any other blemish, but holy and blameless. In this same way, husbands ought to love their wives as their own bodies. He who loves his wife loves himself. After all, no one ever hated his own body, but he feeds and cares for it, just as Christ does the church—for we are members of his body. "For this

reason a man will leave his father and mother and be united to his wife, and the two will become one flesh." This is a profound mystery—but I am talking about Christ and the church. However, each one of you also must love his wife as he loves himself, and the wife must respect her husband (Eph. 5:22–33).

If you are married, does your marriage exemplify God's love? If you are a wife, are you trusting God to lead your husband? If you are a husband, are you loving your wife and sacrificing yourself for her as Christ sacrificed himself for the church?

If you follow God's plan for marriage, your love will deepen and grow—and God may surprise you with unexpected opportunities! I don't know where God will lead John and me as we raise our family and seek to serve him, but I'm excited for the future.

Whether or not you are married, if you are a believer in Christ, you are part of the bride of Christ and can share in the most wondrous and fulfilling love of all. Whitney Houston sang that the "Greatest Love of All" is loving oneself. She was wrong. The greatest love is that which compelled Jesus to give his life for us.

If you have never experienced that love, why not call on him today? Let him surprise you with the depth of his passion for you!

seven

SURPRISED BY CHILDREN

∽

A FEW YEARS AGO I DREAMED I HAD A BABY BOY. HE WAS sitting in my shopping cart at K-Mart. I turned for about thirty seconds to look at something on the shelf. When I turned again, my baby had disappeared. I rushed to the front and told a cashier about my missing boy, but she did not seem to care. Instead of wasting time with her, I looked out the front windows and saw a woman carrying my smiling baby.

As my heart pounded, I ran to her with the speed of an Olympic champion. I grabbed my baby and did a karate chop on the kidnapper, then carried my son to the safety of my car.

Upon waking, I told my husband, John, about my strange dream. John's brown eyes widened. "You won't believe this, Heather. Two nights ago I dreamed we had a baby boy."

Guess what? Two days later I found out I was pregnant. Though I wasn't exactly surprised that I was expecting, I can't say that either John or I had any natural notion of what the gender of this stirring new creation would be. But in good time we saw for ourselves: It was a boy.

We now have two small sons, John and James. John was only nine months old when I discovered I was pregnant again. Now that *was* a surprise! When I first heard that I would be having another baby, I cried—not out of happiness, but for purely selfish reasons. I did not want to lose even more sleep and have yet another baby in diapers! My husband was thrilled about our growing family, but he didn't have to breast-feed every two or three hours all day and all night.

When James was born, John-John (as we call him) was seventeen months old. So now I am a happy mother with two young boys, a busy husband, and an active, fun-loving Labrador. And you know what? I don't mind changing diapers. I know this stage will pass all too quickly, so I will enjoy my babies while I can.

Babies are precious to God even before they are born, and the Bible gives many accounts of God giving people messages of upcoming births. God sent an angel to speak to Hagar about her son, Ishmael, before his birth. He also sent angels to speak to Sarah about her son, Isaac, before he was conceived. The Angel of the Lord (whom many believe to be Jesus) spoke to Manoah about Samson, the son she would bear. Eli assured Hannah that she would have a son, and in time her child, Samuel, became one of Israel's greatest prophets. Another man of God predicted the birth of King Josiah, who rid the Temple of false priests, and Elisha prophesied the birth of a son to a woman who had been childless for years.

S U R P R I S E M E W I T H A B A B Y

I'd like you to consider two births that could be the hands-down winner of a "Surprise Me with a Baby" contest. The first-runner up would be Elizabeth, an infertile older woman, and the undisputed winner would be Mary, a virgin from Nazareth.

Elizabeth conceived first. The wife of a priest named Zechariah, Elizabeth was a good woman who walked with God. But one particular prayer from her heart had not been answered in all the winding length of her marriage. Elizabeth was barren; she could not have children. The Scripture doesn't tell us exactly how old Elizabeth was, but I think we can assume she was well into or nearing menopause, for Luke records that she and Zechariah were "well along in years."

When Zechariah's turn came to serve as priest at the Temple altar, he saw the surprise of his life:

> An angel of the Lord appeared to him, standing at the right side of the altar of incense. When Zechariah saw him, he was startled and was gripped with fear. But the angel said to him: "Do not be afraid, Zechariah; your prayer has been heard. Your wife Elizabeth will bear you a son, and you are to give him the name John. He will be a

LET GOD SURPRISE YOU

joy and delight to you, and many will rejoice
because of his birth, for he will be great in the sight
of the Lord" (Luke 1:11–15).

Hold everything! A *baby?* Zechariah couldn't believe
his ears.

"How can I be sure of this? I am an old man and
my wife is well along in years."
The angel answered, "I am Gabriel. I stand in
the presence of God, and I have been sent to speak
to you and to tell you this good news. And now
you will be silent and not able to speak until the
day this happens, because you did not believe my
words, which will come true at their proper time"
(Luke 1:18–20).

Can't you just see Zechariah coming out of the holy
place and gesturing wildly in his own special sign language?
Zechariah and Elizabeth would have been overjoyed to
conceive an ordinary baby, but this baby would be a great
prophet, preparing the hearts of the people to accept the
coming Messiah.

As the birth date approached, Elizabeth remained in
seclusion, savoring the changes in her waistline. Meanwhile, farther north, in Nazareth, her young niece, Mary,
betrothed to a man named Joseph, heard an even more
amazing message from Gabriel. "The angel went to her and
said, 'Greetings, you who are highly favored! The Lord is
with you'" (Luke 1:28).

Mary was "greatly troubled" and perplexed.

But the angel said to her, "Do not be afraid, Mary, you have found favor with God. You will be with child and give birth to a son, and you are to give him the name Jesus. He will be great and will be called the Son of the Most High. The Lord God will give him the throne of his father David, and he will reign over the house of Jacob forever; his kingdom will never end."

"How will this be," Mary asked the angel, "since I am a virgin?"

The angel answered, "The Holy Spirit will come upon you, and the power of the Most High will overshadow you. So the holy one to be born will be called the Son of God" (Luke 1:30–35).

Gabriel ended his message by telling Mary of Elizabeth's miracle pregnancy. "She who was said to be barren is in her sixth month. For nothing is impossible with God" (1:36–37).

I love this story! Overcome with the news she had heard, Mary bundled some clothing together and traveled south to visit Elizabeth. At the sight of Mary, Elizabeth immediately perceived Mary's condition. The Holy Spirit shared the news and Elizabeth exclaimed, "Blessed are you among women, and blessed is the child you will bear. My baby's turning somersaults because he knows your secret!"

Mary responded with a song of praise:

My soul glorifies the Lord
and my spirit rejoices in God my Savior,
for he has been mindful
of the humble state of his servant (Luke 1:46–48).

Of course "the end" of this story—the birth of Jesus in Bethlehem—is only the beginning of the bigger story of his life and ministry, his redeeming death, his resurrection and ascension to his father. This is also the beginning of a bigger story for Mary as Jesus' mother—a story that involved years of washing soiled clothes, feeding his growing-boy's hunger, worrying about his education and welfare, even about the kinds of friends he chose. The Gospels don't say much about Mary's mothering, but Luke says, "Mary treasured up all these things and pondered them in her heart" (Luke 2:19).

PONDERING MOTHERHOOD

My views of motherhood have changed since my early college days when I was determined to become a successful CPA and perhaps establish my own company. I thought I'd be willing to sacrifice family time for my career, and I planned to put marriage on a back burner, marrying if—and when—it suited my plans. But as I traveled throughout the world and spoke to many successful businesswomen, I learned that they regretted not spending time with their children. Many of them with older children ruefully told me they were too late—by the time they realized what they had done, their children had grown up and were too busy to spend time with their mothers.

I'll never forget an encounter I observed at the Super Bowl in Miami during my term as Miss America. I was in the VIP room along with a few celebrities waiting to participate in the program. One woman had brought along her two children and their nanny. When one of the children began to cry (obviously, the little boy was worn out from all the excitement), the mother offered her comfort. But he didn't want his mom. He walked straight to the nanny and hugged her. I was shocked, and I couldn't help but notice the hurt in the mother's eyes. In that moment, I knew I never wanted my children to see me as anything but their number-one comforter.

Now that I have two boys of my own, I frequently think of wise King Solomon. One night in a dream, God asked Solomon an amazing question: "Ask for whatever you want me to give you."

After thanking God for his faithfulness and kindness, Solomon answered,

> You have made your servant king in place of my father David. But I am only a little child and do not know how to carry out my duties. Your servant is here among the people you have chosen, a great people, too numerous to count or number. So give your servant a discerning heart to govern your people and to distinguish between right and wrong. For who is able to govern this great people of yours? (1 Kings 3:7–9)

Knowing that many people would have asked for long life or riches or victory over his enemies, God was pleased with Solomon's unselfish request. He answered, "I will give you a wise and discerning heart, so that there will never have been anyone like you, nor will there ever be" (1 Kings 3:12).

I know how hard parenting is for mothers and fathers. I have often prayed for the "wisdom of Solomon" as I take care of my little boys. It's so hard to know what is right. How do you discipline properly? When do you say no? I want to be firm but not harsh. I want to love but not spoil them. I need wisdom, and I know I will need more and more as my boys grow older.

But God is faithful, and just as he gave Solomon wisdom and great insight and a breadth of understanding as measureless as the sand on the seashore (1 Kings 4:29), I know he will give me the wisdom I need if I seek him.

I never understood the depths of a mother's love until I had children of my own. And now I cringe at the thought of the court case Solomon was asked to judge: two baby boys—one living and one dead—and two women, both claiming to be the mother of the live baby. Which woman was telling the truth? Wise Solomon understood the depths of a mother's love. To smoke out the liar, he decreed, "Cut the living child in two and give half to one and half to the other" (1 Kings 3:25).

His suggestion was only a ploy, though the women didn't know that. The lying, selfish mother said, "Fine. Let both babies die." The mother who was telling the truth saw things differently. She begged for the baby to be saved— even if it meant that he would go to the other woman. Her baby's life was more important than her happiness.

Now that I have children, I understand that mother's sacrificial love. Because I want to be available to them, I have decided to accept fewer outside engagements and stay at home more. After all, what does it matter if the world praises my accomplishments? My children need to know that I care deeply for them. That's far more important. Some people invest money in stocks to make more money; I invest time in my family to glorify God. In return, God blesses me with opportunities that reach more people when I do go out while he allows me to guard my family time.

Thomas Jefferson once said, "He does best in God's great world who does his best in his own little world."[1] If I can do my best with my children and my husband, I'll be doing my part to fulfill God's plan for the world at large.

I have dreams for my children—the two boys I have now, and the other children I'd like to have some day. I want my boys to consider us—John and me—their best friends and mentors throughout their lives. I want them to know how much we love them and that we are there to support them.

Of course, I do enjoy imagining what my boys might be like as adults. Their personalities are so different. If, for instance, they both went into the military, John would probably be an Air Force pilot because he thinks twice before he does something. James, on the other hand, would probably be either a Navy SEAL or a Marine because he will tackle almost anything like it's no big deal.

Most important, I want my children to have a relationship with Jesus. I know sometimes I will disappoint them, but Jesus never will. He is my role model for overcoming problems and my forever loving friend. If Jesus can be those things to me, I know he can be the same things to my boys.

CHILDREN AS TREASURED GIFTS

At the beginning of the chapter I talked about miracle children of the Bible, supernatural gifts from God. Sometimes we tend to forget that *every* child is a gift from God. Psalm 127:3 says,

> Sons are a heritage from the Lord,
> children a reward from him.

The prophetic books of Jeremiah and Isaiah, as well as the Psalms, talk of God's plans for children even while they are in the womb. "Before I formed you in the womb I knew you," God said to Jeremiah (1:5). Isaiah 44:2 refers to God as "he who made you, who formed you in the womb."

As gifts from God, our children—whether they come to us by plan or by surprise—need to be treasured and protected. You don't have to worry; God's timing is always perfect. As the Bible says, "There is a time for everything, and a season for every activity under heaven" (Eccl. 3:1).

TRUSTING GOD WITH HEARTBREAK

If God surprises you with an unexpected child, you can trust his timing even if his plan brings you heartbreak. I don't know Nancy Guthrie personally, but a friend of mine does, and I've heard about her incredible story.

In 1998, Nancy and her husband, parents of a ten-year-old son, discovered that their newborn baby girl, Hope, had Zellweger syndrome, a rare congenital disorder. Faced with the prognosis that Hope would live no more than six months, the family took Hope home and loved her as best

they could through her short life. To prevent future pregnancies, Nancy's husband had a vasectomy.

Imagine their surprise and apprehension eighteen months
later when Nancy became pregnant again. Although there
was only a 25 percent chance the baby would carry the
disease, prenatal tests indicated that this child was also a
Zellweger baby.

Nancy did not abort the boy. Again, the family brought
the new baby, Gabriel, home and loved him until his death,
one day short of his six-month birthday.

In her book *Holding on to Hope,* Nancy says her decision to trust in God is a daily choice, not a one-time action,
and she has difficult days like anyone else. She is honest
about her agonizing sorrow and pain.[2] She is also honest
about how hard it is to trust God with shattered dreams:

> Since Hope's death, I have had to let go of her
> physical body, my dreams for her, and many of her
> things. I have had to let go of her room and turn it
> back into a guest room. I have a sweet friend who
> put together a beautiful scrapbook of Hope's life.
> Another friend who saw the scrapbook said to me,
> "I know what you would grab first in a fire!" . . .
> I've realized that I have to be willing to let go of
> that book, too. To some that may seem a silly sac-
> rifice, but the book represents all my memories of
> Hope. I have to hold on to those loosely as well.[3]

The key to Nancy's emotional survival lies in her realization that everything she has—her possessions, her husband,
her children—is a gift from God. And we should be grateful

for gifts, no matter how long we have them. Through her struggle and her grief, Nancy and her husband have realized one important thing: God is enough.

> I did not want to lose Hope. I would have liked to watch her grow. I would have liked to have known her as an adult, to have had a grown daughter who looked like me and talked like me to be my friend in my old age. But I also know that this life is filled with pain, and I don't believe it is a tragedy that Hope had the opportunity to be spared from the evil and pain of this life and instead be in the presence of God.
>
> That is what I believe. It is not necessarily how I feel. But my belief does make a difference in how I feel.[4]

Whether or not you have lost a child, you may have suffered the loss of a broken dream. Just as the Guthries have entrusted Hope and Gabriel to the tender care of Jesus, you can trust the Lord with your shattered dreams. He does not bring suffering into our lives without a purpose. Everything that happens to a child of God—whether good or bad—comes through the hand of our loving Father and is designed to help us become more like Christ.

TRUSTING GOD WITH A CHILD'S UNCERTAIN FUTURE

Christian novelist Kristin Billerbeck, author of *Heirloom Brides* and many other novellas, had three closely spaced boys before she was surprised by an unexpected pregnancy. "I was done with bringing children into our family," she says. "Three was good. With one special-needs child and my own battle with multiple sclerosis, I didn't want to test myself further. Although my husband desired four children and had actually said, 'I feel there's someone missing from our family portrait,' he agreed to a vasectomy after his friends jokingly asked if he was insane to want more children.

"The day of his vasectomy, I felt positively giddy with relief. After three children, I was done. Now I could concentrate on their well-being and triumphantly move out of the diaper phase.

"When my husband, Bryed, came home from the appointment, he looked scared. 'I had the appointment wrong,' he told me. 'It wasn't the third at two P.M. It was the second at three—yesterday.'"

A month passed before Kristin's husband could get another appointment. By then, she had felt the familiar emotions she usually associated with pregnancy. The missed doctor's appointment resulted in significant repercussions.

Kristin passed the first four months of her pregnancy in a fog. The coming baby didn't seem real, but then God surprised her again. "At five months, we had an ultrasound. We never doubted that the baby would be our fourth son. Apple trees produce apples; we produce boys. The day of the ultrasound, my husband went skiing and I went to the doctor's office alone. The front desk nurse said, 'Well, it's a girl day. We've had all girls today.'

"'I'll break your streak,' I told her. 'I only have boys. This will be my fourth.' Off I went in to see the technician, and after a short time he said, 'It's a girl.'"

"'It's a boy,' I countered. 'Check again.' I didn't want a girl. I liked being a boy mom; it had become a big part of my identity. I didn't want a whiny girl (another me) in the house! The technician showed me in graphic detail why he thought this baby was a girl, but I still didn't believe him."

Because Kristin's MS flared at the end of her pregnancy, her doctor decided to induce labor two weeks early. She was so convinced she was having another son that she went into the labor room without even picking out a girl's name.

But . . . it was a girl. "She was beautiful and I loved her immediately. Suddenly, I desperately wanted a girl. *This* girl."

Little Elle is now two years old. "She's my little best friend," Kristin says. "She loves to shop and cuddle and dance. I can't describe the depth of the mother-daughter bond we share.

"If I'd been allowed to control my destiny, I would have never known this gift that God saved for me. On her birth announcement, I wrote, 'I sing for joy at the work of your hands.' There is nothing better to describe my utter amazement at the work of God in Elle's life. She did not walk until eighteen months; at two she still struggles with speech."

Kristin herself has a degenerative disease and her son has special needs. Just as she didn't know God's plan for her—as a mother of a young daughter—she doesn't know what God has in store for her Elle. Even so, she says, "I wouldn't have missed it (this surprise birth) for anything." There's no such thing as a "mistake" child.[5]

Looking Back with Delight

Deborah Raney, author of novels such as *A Vow to Cherish,* was utterly surprised with what she delightfully calls a "bonus baby." She had always dreamed of having a large family: twelve children—six biological offspring and six more by adoption. But by time she was college age, doctors warned her that she might not be able to bear any children. "That didn't concern me in the least," she says, "I just decided that I'd adopt all twelve."

To the doctors' amazement, she and her husband Ken had three children over the course of six years. She says, "Our three children are proof that sometimes God intervenes in miraculous ways. Most days three children seemed like twelve, and we were beyond content with the little family God had given us.

"I was privileged to be a stay-at-home mom, and since we would have been happy with another baby, we chose not to use any kind of birth control."

As the oldest child entered high school, Deborah started to think about getting an outside job to help with college expenses. No longer entertaining the idea of a surprise baby, she gathered brochures on vasectomies and tubal ligation. "While Ken and I discussed which one of us should have the surgery, the Lord had a better idea—her name is Tavia Amber, and she is the joy of our lives."

I'll let Deborah finish the story in her own words:

> I wish I could say we immediately embraced the news of my fourth pregnancy and joyfully accepted

that there would be another little pair of feet pattering about our floors. It wasn't that easy. We'd thought those middle-of-the-night feedings were behind us. We'd thought the days of toy-littered floors and burp-stained shoulders were over. Our kids were finally to the point where we could leave them home on a Saturday night and spend a glorious evening on the town, just the two of us. And now . . . I was pregnant again.

I spent about two weeks vacillating between depression and amazement. Then I thought about how quickly our other babies had grown up, and I remembered my childhood dream of raising twelve children. I said, "Okay. Thank you, Lord!"

As the weeks went by and I started reading up on pregnancy and babies again, suddenly I couldn't think of anything I'd rather be doing than bringing this precious little life into the world.

I won't deny that getting used to the idea of having a baby in the house again was a huge adjustment. Our children were all settled in school, and I was excited about going back to college or finding a job outside the home. Our financial need was extreme, and we couldn't imagine how we could feed another mouth, let alone help the older kids with college.

It's amazing how the things we worry about seem so insignificant after the Lord has intervened. He provided every need in our lives. I decided to try my hand at writing—a dream I'd held since childhood. I began writing on New Year's Day 1994, and eight months later I was offered a book contract for an amount that was, to the penny, the amount we'd just been told our oldest son's four years at college (room, board, and tuition) would cost!

Not only did God work out the technical aspects of adding another baby to our family, but with every passing year we see another wonderful facet of God's intervention. Tavia's birth presented growth opportunities for each of our other children. In fact, I'm almost certain she is the reason our oldest daughter became a teacher. And each of her big football-playing brothers developed a precious tender streak as a result of caring for a baby. Tavia has also opened doors in Ken's and my life to rich friendships with couples much younger than we are. We believe she has kept us young.[6]

I wanted to share Deborah's perspective, as she is older than I and can look back on that surprise pregnancy from a distance that shows some of the good results of God's gift of a fourth child, even at what seemed to be such an inopportune time.

ONE MOMENT AT A TIME

Believe me, I know that for a mother any day can bring unimaginable surprises—both celebratory and worrisome. I'm learning that there is only one way to face the day— one little moment at a time. Earlier in the chapter I quoted Thomas Jefferson. I wonder if Jefferson had read the earlier writer Blaise Pascal, whose *Pensees,* or fragmentary ponderings, were collected and published after his death. A few lines of Pascal remind me of Jefferson's quote—and the idea it presents helps me trust God as I face each day of wiping noses and washing t-shirts. "Do the little things as though they were great, because of the majesty of Jesus Christ who does them in us and lives in our life."[7] Maybe that's the message we mothers need most to hear. Because of what Christ has done for us, we should do the little things as if they were great. Whether we are changing diapers or cheering at high school football games, we can rejoice in our children, our gifts from God, and trust the Lord with the surprises he brings.

eight

SURPRISED BY
PROVISION

~

FOOD FOR ELIJAH

Elijah the Tishbite is one of the most colorful characters in Scripture. He first appears in the Bible as a rugged wilderness man; we know nothing about his youth or his parents.

We first see Elijah standing before the wicked King Ahab. Without thought for his own safety, Elijah denounces the king for leading the Israelites in idol worship. As God's judgment upon the people, Elijah announced, there would be "neither dew nor rain in the next few years except at my word" (1 Kings 17:1).

Pretty bold pronouncement, wasn't it? Ahab didn't believe Elijah at first, but as the crops dried up, cattle died, and people began to starve, the king turned his thoughts to the troublesome prophet—and sought ways to kill him. To escape Ahab's wrath, Elijah, at God's direction, retreated to a brook that provided him water to drink. And there, every day, morning and night, God provided bread and meat for Elijah—delivered by special air transport: a band of flying ravens.

We don't know how long this provision lasted. Scripture simply says that "some time later the brook dried up" (1 Kings 17:7). At that point God told Elijah to go to a little town called Zarephath and look for a particular widow who would give him food.

Elijah recognized the widow gathering sticks and greeted her. "Hello, ma'am. Nice to meet you. Now, if you'd please bring me a cup of water and a little bit of bread, I'd appreciate it."

Sounds pretty brazen, doesn't it? We don't typically drive up to strangers' houses and invite ourselves in for dinner, but in the desert settlements of those days, it was customary to offer food and drink to travelers. Life depended on such hospitality.

The widow shook her head when he asked for food.

> "As surely as the Lord your God lives," she replied, "I don't have any bread—only a handful of flour in a jar and a little oil in a jug. I am gathering a few sticks to take home and make a meal for myself and my son, that we may eat it—and die" (1 Kings 17:12).

It is obvious that this beleaguered woman recognized Elijah as a prophet, but she seems to have no personal faith in the God of Israel. At that moment, I doubt she believed in much of anything; starvation and despair had defeated her hope. She offered Elijah all she felt she could—respect and honesty, telling him that she was going home to prepare for herself and her son one last meal before waiting to die.

The prophet's next words are a resounding scriptural message for people blessed by God: "Don't be afraid." And then Elijah makes a surprising request: Gather your wood, go home, and start to cook.

> "But first make a small cake of bread for me from what you have and bring it to me, and then make something for yourself and your son. For this is what the Lord, the God of Israel, says: 'The jar of flour will not be used up and the jug of oil will not run dry until the day the Lord gives rain on the land.'"
>
> She went away and did as Elijah had told her. So there was food every day for Elijah and for the woman and her family. For the jar of flour was not used up and the jug of oil did not run dry, in keeping with the word of the Lord spoken by Elijah (1 Kings 17:13–16).

Now that's what I call living by faith! Every day this poor widow went to her pantry, pulled out the jar of oil and the jug of flour, and doled out enough to make what probably looked like three flat pancakes, which she shared with the prophet and her son. And every day that meager meal sustained them another twenty-four hours. Day by day she sheltered the prophet in her upstairs room, she made her small cakes, and they survived.

But the God of surprising provision had not won her heart. That happens in the next part of the story. After Elijah had been staying in the attic room awhile, the widow's son got sick, so sick that he "stopped breathing." Understandably upset, the woman called Elijah to the bedside. She couldn't believe what was happening, and she blamed Elijah: "What do you have against me, man of God? Did you come to remind me of my sin and kill my son?" (1 Kings 17:18)

Elijah responded coolly, calmly, kindly. "'Give me your son,' Elijah replied. He took him from her arms, carried him to the upper room where he was staying, and laid him on his bed" (17:19).

Elijah himself was surprised and turned to God with a hard question and a faith-filled request:

> Then he cried out to the Lord, "O Lord my God, have you brought tragedy also upon this widow I am staying with, by causing her son to die?" Then he stretched himself out on the boy three times and cried to the Lord, "O Lord my God, let this boy's life return to him!"
>
> The Lord heard Elijah's cry, and the boy's life returned to him, and he lived. Elijah picked up the child and carried him down from the room into the house. He gave him to his mother and said, "Look, your son is alive!" (1 Kings 17:20–23).

The biblical writer gave one more detail of the widow's story. Seeing this last life-giving miracle, her doubt turned to belief. "Then the woman said to Elijah, 'Now I know that you are a man of God and that the word of the Lord from your mouth is the truth'" (17:24).

That may be the end of the biblical story of the widow of Zarephath (though Jesus himself would later refer to her), but God would again provide Elijah with bread and water when he was exhausted and weak in the desert (1 Kings 19:5-8).

VITAMINS FOR CORRIE

God is still capable of miraculously supplying the needs of his people. You may be familiar with the story of Corrie (Cornelia) ten Boom, the Dutch woman who helped hide Jews during the Nazi oppression of Haarlem. Corrie's father, Casper ten Boom, owned and operated a jewelry store in the heart of the city's Jewish quarter. A devout Christian, Casper believed the Jews were God's chosen people; he even studied the Talmud and participated with his Jewish neighbors in their Sabbath and holy day celebrations.

Corrie was the youngest child of three girls and one son born to Casper and his wife. The ten Booms were a close-knit family, studying the Bible and praying together every day.

When the Nazis began to persecute Jews in Haarlem, Corrie and her family decided to do what they could to help, becoming a pivotal part of a network helping Jews escape to safer countries.

In the privacy of her room, Corrie prayed, "Lord Jesus, I offer myself for your people. In any way. Any place. Any time." The family's mission involved building a secret room in Corrie's bedroom in which they could hide—and save—Jews in danger. But in February 1944, Corrie, her father, and siblings were arrested. Corrie's courageous father lived only ten days in Scheveningen Prison. Corrie spent four months in solitary confinement, then eventually was transferred to Ravensbruck with her older sister, Betsie.

In Ravensbruck, a place of horrendous, unimaginable suffering, God worked miracles to sustain the sisters' courage. The miracles began on the first day. Horror filled Corrie when she realized that guards stripped all arriving prisoners of everything they owned—clothing, purses, possessions. She worried about Betsie losing her warm sweater, for the climate was cold. She worried about losing her little bottle of liquid vitamins, for vitamin deficiency, coupled with malnutrition, meant certain illness. But sheer panic gripped her when she thought about losing the small Bible she wore in a pouch hung on a string-necklace. For many days the Word of God had comforted and consoled her, and she had shared its hope with others. Would it now be confiscated?

Bibles were forbidden in the camp. Being caught with one meant an instant doubling of the prison term and a halving of all rations. Though Corrie knew the high risk involved, she clung to her Bible.

Standing in line, waiting for the command to strip and drop all possessions, Corrie boldly asked for permission to use the bathroom. There, wrapping the Bible and her little vitamin bottle in Betsie's sweater, she placed the bundle behind a pile of cockroach-ridden benches. Later, after Corrie and Betsie had put on the regulation uniforms, Corrie hid the precious bundle under her dress.

In her book *The Hiding Place*, she describes the scene with characteristic wry humor:

> [The bundle] made a bulge you could have seen across the Grote Markt. I flattened it out as best I could, pushing it down, tugging the sweater around my waist, but there was no real concealing it beneath the thin cotton dress. And all the while I had the incredible feeling that it didn't matter, that this was not my business, but God's. That all I had to do was walk straight ahead.[1]

Confidently, she approached the guards. The S.S. men ran their hands over every woman in line; they investigated every bulge and lump. They searched the woman in front of Corrie three times. They searched Betsie, who walked behind Corrie. But Corrie passed by the guards without being noticed, as if no one could see her in the line. When she passed by a second row of guards at the door, the guard in charge shoved her forward and told her to hurry up. But she was not searched. So the Bible and the vitamins made it safely through the line of probing guards.

Vitamin deficiency was one of the worst problems facing the prisoners, and Corrie's first instinct was to reserve the vitamins for her emaciated, sick sister. But others were sick too, and Corrie couldn't ignore their feverish eyes and refuse their trembling hands. Soon more than twenty-five women were receiving a daily dose of vitamins.

> Every time I tilted the little bottle, a drop appeared at the tip of the glass stopper. It just couldn't be! I held it up to the light, trying to see how much was

left, but the dark brown glass was too thick to see through.

"There was a woman in the Bible," Betsie said, "whose oil jar was never empty." ... Well—but—wonderful things happened all through the Bible. It was one thing to believe that such things were possible thousands of years ago, another to have it happen now, to us, this very day. And yet it happened this day, and the next, and the next, until an awed little group of spectators stood around watching the drops fall onto the daily rations of bread.

Many nights I lay awake in the shower of straw dust from the mattress above, trying to fathom the marvel of supply lavished upon us.[2]

Just as God supplied oil and flour for Elijah and the widow, he supplied vitamins for generous Corrie and her fellow prisoners.

The drops lasted until the day a prison-hospital worker smuggled a bag of vitamins to Corrie. And that night, when Corrie opened her own vitamin bottle, she found the container empty. However, the new supply of vitamins filled the need for weeks to come.

Do you notice the common link between Corrie's story and the widow's? God's surprise provision came as women generously shared what little they had with others. The widow could have refused Elijah's request for water and food. She could have insisted that she had just enough for herself and her son. Likewise, Corrie could have hoarded her vitamins for herself and her ailing sister. But she chose to extend compassion and love in the form of vitamin drops.

In both situations, God proved himself faithful by rewarding those with generous hearts.

"Give," Jesus said, "and it will be given to you. A good measure, pressed down, shaken together and running over, will be poured into your lap. For with the measure you use, it will be measured to you" (Luke 6:38).

E N L A R G E   M Y   K I N G D O M   W O R K

A few months ago I read *The Prayer of Jabez* in which Bruce Wilkinson explains that God honored Jabez because he prayed, "Oh, that you would bless me and enlarge my territory!" (1 Chron. 4:10)

While I was reading Wilkinson's book, John and I were looking for a larger family house with a bigger yard for the boys to play in. We made three offers on three different houses, but were turned down each time. After searching six more months, we found a charming Dutch colonial house on two acres. I loved it. It seemed perfect. But the asking price was beyond our planned budget. The seller would not reduce the price, and we had to make a decision. Buy or let it go.

I thought of Jabez and prayed, "Lord, please enlarge my territory because I want to increase our family someday and have a bigger ministry if it is your will. Also let me serve you more through my career in order to continue to bring light to the world in Jesus' name."

I was thinking of maybe writing more books and having a few more speaking appearances. Then, to my surprise, through two book contracts, God provided us with the financial support to buy a sweet home. Because God has been generous to me, it is my hope and prayer that I will not only have a better place to raise my children, but I will be willing and able to enlarge my personal ministry by serving others.

WANT VERSUS NEED?

I wouldn't want you to think that the Christian life is one of constant abundance. Sometimes God teaches us great faith and patience when we don't get what we want. But he has promised to supply what we *need,* and there's a vast difference between wanting and needing.

A few months ago I received a phone call from a TV production company. They asked if I was interested in acting in a new TV show they were planning for the coming fall. I had not been searching for an acting job, even though I have received other inquiries from TV companies and even a Broadway show. I immediately said no to those previous queries, because I did not want to compromise my Christian faith. I had not believed it possible for a deaf actress to find work in a show with Christian values.

Then God surprised me with this opportunity. I felt so honored. I thought the part was perfect for me. I fell in love with the show concept about a deaf Christian woman. What an opportunity to minister to thousands around the country and perhaps even around the world.

My heart was hungry and I was ready to go. I was certain God would bless me with this role. Then, to my complete astonishment, the role was given to another woman.

I could not understand. Hadn't God understood how perfect I was for the part? How could he have gotten his wires crossed like that? Surely there was some mistake!

No, God does not make mistakes. I knew this. Even so, I walked around in a funk for about three weeks. As always, God comforted my heart through the Bible, reminding me that he had always taken good care of my family. I looked at our new home and my beautiful boys playing beside our crazy chocolate-brown Labrador retriever, and I remembered how God had answered my prayers. As I focused on gratitude for his provision, I forgot how disappointed I was about losing that TV role. I went down to the basement and praised God by dancing a ballet solo for him alone.

When you lose an opportunity to see a dream come true, take time to look at how many fulfilled dreams you already hold in your hand. Be thankful and go on, knowing that God has a better plan for you.

GOD'S GOOD GIFTS

Have you a need for provision in your own life? Do you need food, clothing, money, or health? God is not a money tree or a Wal-Mart; he does not supply on demand. But he is willing, even happy, to give good gifts to his children when they ask in his will and with a humble heart.

Jesus told us:

> Ask and it will be given to you; seek and you will find; knock and the door will be opened to you. For everyone who asks receives; he who seeks finds; and to him who knocks, the door will be opened.

Which of you, if his son asks for bread, will give
him a stone? Or if he asks for a fish, will give him
a snake? If you, then, though you are evil, know
how to give good gifts to your children, how much
more will your Father in heaven give good gifts to
those who ask him! (Matthew 7:7–11)

And James 1:17 says, "Every good and perfect gift is
from above, coming down from the Father of the heavenly
lights, who does not change like shifting shadows." We are
not always able to know what good God is planning to
work in and through our lives. Despite Corrie's vitamins,
her sister Betsie died in Ravensbruck. But within days,
Corrie was inexplicably released from the camp. After
regaining her strength—at an age when Americans start
thinking about retirement—she began working to fulfill a
dream she and Betsie had envisioned: setting up a ministry
to help people who had been wounded and displaced in the
war. Only years later, on a visit to Ravensbruck, did Corrie
learn that she had been released because of a clerical error.
A week after her release, all the female prisoners her age
had been sent to the gas chambers.

God provided for Corrie, and even Betsie, in more ways
than she realized at the time. He surprised her, just as he
surprised the widow of Zarephath with new oil and even a
resuscitated son—and he will surprise you if you generously
open your heart.

nine

SURPRISED BY

MINISTRY

‿

HIS ENEMIES CALLED HIM A TROUBLEMAKER, A BABBLER, A defiler, insane, a murderer—or a god. His friends called him a dear brother. We who look back on him from the perspective of twenty centuries see him as a scholar, a sage, a seer, and a saint; a Christian statesman, an organizational genius, a visionary, a loving pastor, a great preacher, a profound theologian, a persuasive apologist, and a master builder of the church. We marvel at his keen intellect and profound mysticism. We ponder his ailing, scarred body and are astonished at his enormous capacity for hard work.

He may be attacked or defended, but millions read every day from his writings. He's the first-century giant we know as the apostle Paul.[1]

PAUL'S ABOUT-FACE

The first time Scripture mentions the man we know as the apostle Paul, he goes by his Jewish name Saul and is a mere postscript to another man's story. Stephen, a deacon in the early days in the first church in Jerusalem, is described as "a man full of God's grace and power" who "did great wonders and miraculous signs among the people" (Acts 6:8). Because he stood his ground when staunch Jewish opponents debated with him, they accused him of blasphemy.

> So they stirred up the people and the elders and the teachers of the law. They seized Stephen and brought him before the Sanhedrin. They produced false witnesses, who testified, "This fellow never stops speaking against this holy place and against the law. For we have heard him say that this Jesus of Nazareth will destroy this place and change the customs Moses handed down to us."
>
> All who were sitting in the Sanhedrin looked intently at Stephen, and they saw that his face was like the face of an angel (Acts 6:12–15).

Stephen then gave one of the most powerful testimonies about God's plan for the Hebrew people recorded in Scripture. But his hearers' hearts were hardened to the truth. His sincere conviction infuriated them so much that they "dragged him out of the city and began to stone him." This is where we first see Saul. "Meanwhile, the witnesses laid their clothes at the feet of a young man named Saul" (Acts 7:58).

As Stephen died he repeated the incredible prayer of Jesus on the cross: "'Lord, do not hold this sin against them.' When he had said this, he fell asleep" (Acts 7:60).

The author of Acts then segues into the fascinating story of Saul, who would soon be known as Paul:

> And Saul was there, giving approval to his death.
> On that day a great persecution broke out against the church at Jerusalem, and all except the apostles were scattered throughout Judea and Samaria. Godly men buried Stephen and mourned deeply for him. But Saul began to destroy the church. Going from house to house, he dragged off men and women and put them in prison (Acts 8:1–3).

This young Saul was not what we'd call a purposeless hoodlum. He was an educated and devout Jew, born into an influential family in the city of Tarsus in Asia Minor, under Roman rule. His father was a Pharisee, the strictest sect of the Jews. He was brought up from a youth to be faultless in legalistic righteousness (Phil. 3:6). Wanting to be a teacher of the law, he traveled from Tarsus to Jerusalem, to study with the renowned Rabbi Gamaliel, memorizing the scriptures and debating their meaning with other religious intellectuals. And he was still in Jerusalem when followers of Jesus, "the Nazarene," began to claim that their long-awaited Messiah had risen from the dead.

Saul may not have thrown a stone at Stephen, but he obviously approved of the killing and thereafter became a ringleader in rounding up and imprisoning believers. He hoped the sect would die away. But it didn't. Some believers fled the city, taking their faith with them and sowing seeds of belief in Jesus across the world. The Christians who remained in Jerusalem looked death in the eye and merely cocked a brow. Stephen hadn't been afraid to die, and neither were they.

You might say that young Saul, eager to show his religious devotion, signed on for police detail, "breathing out murderous threats against the Lord's disciples" (Acts 9:1). Hearing that many believers were hiding in Damascus, he asked the high priest for a letter of introduction so the Jewish leaders in Damascus would give him access to local Jews who believed in "the Way," as the Christian sect was then called. The high priest gave his approval and Saul set off.

Damascus was a six-day journey from Jerusalem, and I imagine Saul's anger burned hotter with every step he took. He would find those Christians, he would put them in prison, and then they'd see what happened to people who flouted the law of God.

That's when Saul ran headlong into the surprise of his life: He met the One in whom he had stubbornly refused to believe.

> As he neared Damascus on his journey, suddenly a light from heaven flashed around him. He fell to the ground and heard a voice say to him, "Saul, Saul, why do you persecute me?"
>
> "Who are you, Lord?" Saul asked.
>
> "I am Jesus, whom you are persecuting," he replied. "Now get up and go into the city, and you will be told what you must do."

The men traveling with Saul stood there speech-
less; they heard the sound but did not see anyone.
Saul got up from the ground, but when he opened
his eyes he could see nothing. So they led him by
the hand into Damascus (Acts 9:3–8).

Saul's glimpse of the glorified One left him temporarily
blind and thoroughly humiliated. For three days he sat in
darkness, unable to eat or drink. I imagine he did little but
think about the terrible things he had done to Christians and
how he had wasted his life trying to follow the law in order
to please God. The Bible tells us he prayed—probably for
strength, sight, and forgiveness.

On the third day the Holy Spirit told Ananias, a Jewish believer in Damascus, to go to a certain house and ask
for Saul of Tarsus by name. Apprehensive but obedient,
Ananias found Saul, prayed for him to receive his sight, and
baptized him as a symbol of his conversion.

Saul's life would never be the same. His encounter with
the risen Lord would bring about a new mind-set, a new
name, and a new mandate for ministry. The Spirit told
Ananias, "This man is my chosen instrument to carry my
name before the Gentiles and their kings and before the
people of Israel" (Acts 9:15).

Immediately Paul started preaching, first in Damascus
and then in Jerusalem. When his life was threatened by the
people who once had been his cohorts, his new Christian
brothers shipped him off to his hometown of Tarsus.

We lose track of Paul for a while, but then a church
leader named Barnabas helps him launch a life-long ministry

as a church planter and evangelist. Paul testified to the power of Christ before kings and governors. He preached in places as far away as Macedonia, Malta, and Rome. For his efforts he was beaten, stoned, shipwrecked, imprisoned, starved, maligned, and misunderstood.

Paul's complete story is too complex to detail here, but I'd like to zoom in on Paul's experience in the city of Philippi. There Paul and Silas preached the message of Christ, and as they made their way from place to place, they were followed by a young woman possessed by an evil spirit. She distracted the crowd with her crying out, but the words she proclaimed were the truth: "These men are servants of the Most High God, who are telling you the way to be saved" (Acts 16:17).

Grieved by her distractions, Paul turned to her and commanded the spirit to leave her. It did, freeing the girl from the evil spirit's domination, but displeasing the men who had profitably used her for fortune-telling. Her masters complained to the city leaders, accusing Paul and Silas of "troubling the city." Paul and Silas were beaten and cast into jail.

Then our surprising God used his servants' misfortune for his glory:

> About midnight Paul and Silas were praying and singing hymns to God, and the other prisoners were listening to them. Suddenly there was such a violent earthquake that the foundations of the prison were shaken. At once all the prison doors flew open, and everybody's chains came loose. The jailer woke up, and when he saw the prison doors open, he drew his

sword and was about to kill himself because he thought the prisoners had escaped. But Paul shouted, "Don't harm yourself! We are all here!"

The jailer called for lights, rushed in and fell trembling before Paul and Silas. He then brought them out and asked, "Sirs, what must I do to be saved?"

They replied, "Believe in the Lord Jesus, and you will be saved—you and your household" (Acts 16:25–31).

As Ananias had baptized Paul, Paul baptized the Philippian jailer—just as we should minister to others because someone once ministered to us.

Through all the hardships he faced, Paul's faith never wavered. As he wrote,

> In all these things we are more than conquerors through him who loved us. For I am convinced that neither death nor life, neither angels nor demons, neither the present nor the future, nor any powers, neither height nor depth, nor anything else in all creation, will be able to separate us from the love of God that is in Christ Jesus our Lord (Rom. 8:37–39).

If Paul, who faced more trials and tests than most of us ever will, could face the future with unshakable faith in God's perfect love, how much more should you and I be able to do so?

When God surprises us with heartache . . .

When we are stunned by loss . . .

When life takes a sharp turn we didn't expect, we can be like Paul, who knew that everything that came his way came through the loving hands of the Father.

Sometimes God allows pain to teach us.

Sometimes he allows hurt to mature us.

Job knew more suffering than most of us will ever experience, and he wrote, "For [God] wounds, but he also binds up; he injures, but his hands also heal" (Job 5:18).

In the latter part of his ministry, Paul wrote his younger friend Timothy, summarizing his life in the framework of thanks to God who *appointed* him for service and allowed him to be an example for men and women who would believe through Paul's witness.

> I thank Christ Jesus our Lord, who has given me strength, that he considered me faithful, appointing me to his service. Even though I was once a blasphemer and a persecutor and a violent man, I was shown mercy because I acted in ignorance and unbelief. The grace of our Lord was poured out on me abundantly, along with the faith and love that are in Christ Jesus.
>
> Here is a trustworthy saying that deserves full acceptance: Christ Jesus came into the world to save sinners—of whom I am the worst. But for that very reason I was shown mercy so that in me, the worst of sinners, Christ Jesus might display his unlimited patience as an example for those who would believe on him and receive eternal life (1 Tim. 1:12–16).

FROM THE FIRST CENTURY TO THE TWENTIETH

You have probably heard of the PAX Network or Home Shopping Network, but you may not be familiar with the man behind them both—Lowell "Bud" Paxon. Like Paul, Paxon met the Lord and was then surprised to discover a new purpose in life.

In 1977 Paxon owned an AM radio station on Florida's west coast. Faced with declining listeners and delinquent advertisers, one afternoon Paxon realized he had to take drastic action to meet payroll. He drove to the office of an appliance dealer who owed him a thousand dollars.

The appliance dealer was less than happy to be reminded of his debt, and he said he wasn't going to pay for advertising that hadn't been effective. In a moment of inspiration, he grinned and said, "I'm overstocked with electric can openers. I have 112 I'd like to get rid of. You can take them as payment in full."[2]

What could Paxon do? He had a choice: take the can openers or walk out with nothing.

So he loaded his van with boxes of can openers. The next morning he walked into the station, saw the stacks of can openers, and heard the voice of his morning radio personality on the air. In a flash point moment he opened the studio door and called, "You've got a guest on your show this morning."

How do you turn down the station owner? The radio host agreed, and a few moments later Paxon was telling the morning listeners that he had an irresistible deal to offer them: Rival can openers, which usually retailed for $14.95, could be had for $9.75 each if buyers came to the station with cash in hand before noon.

Fifteen minutes later, all 112 can openers had been sold.

Paxon's experience with the can openers proved to be a life-changing event. After that he sold all sorts of merchandise on the radio, and within a few years another idea occurred: Why not do the same thing on television? With Roy Speer, with whom he had co-owned an FM station, Paxon launched the Home Shopping Network. Though marketing experts of every ilk predicted the venture was doomed to failure, the shopping network did twelve million dollars in business in the first year. They doubled that amount in the second, and in 1990, eight years after HSN's beginning, sales passed one billion dollars.

But all was not going so well in Bud Paxon's personal life. On Christmas morning in 1986, he opened presents with his family, then followed his wife out onto the lanai because she had asked to speak to him privately.

While they sat on the patio, Paxon's wife said three words he thought he would never hear: "I'm leaving you." Shortly afterward, she packed up her presents and left the house.

In his book *Threading the Needle*, Paxon writes of the experience with honesty:

> My children had all gone back to their homes and I was in a house filled with presents—all alone. I had negotiated deals that changed the way people shop—but I was alone. I had traveled the world—

yet I was alone. I was rich—but I was alone. I had expensive cars and a luxurious house—but I was alone.

In that moment I realized my life had become totally empty. As that truth sank in, I placed my face in my hands and cried. For hours I wept.

I was absolutely and completely bankrupt. I was a millionaire, yet all of my success was worthless because I had lost my wife and wasn't close to my kids.

If I had possessed some sort of spiritual under-pinnings, I might have withstood the blast. Or things might never have gotten so bad. But I didn't.[3]

As part of their Christmas celebration that year, Paxon and his children had planned to go to Las Vegas; of course, he had planned for his wife to go as well. Despite his aching heart, he yielded to the wishes of his children and flew to Las Vegas to spend time with them.

On New Year's Eve, after celebrating with his children, Paxon walked into his Caesar's Palace hotel suite and sank into a chair. Despite his success, his money, and his ambition, he had come to the end of himself and found ... emptiness.

At 4 A.M. Bud Paxon got out of that chair and began to search for the Word of God. After opening thirty-five drawers, he finally found a Bible:

I simply opened it and read what was on the page. Amazingly, the Bible opened to Job, chapter five. I read the story about how God could rescue Job from hardships and troubles and said, "Wow, that's my life."

I then turned to the front of the Bible and found the pages that directed me to the verses that would show me how to find peace with God. It was then that I discovered my sins had separated me from God. It wasn't that I was worse than the next guy, or as bad as I could be, but I knew I had thought, said, and done things that displeased God. And because of that I wasn't worthy to enter his presence. This truth didn't come as a big shock to me. I never thought of myself as a saint and I certainly wasn't religious.[4]

Paxon then turned to Romans 5:8 and read words penned by Paul himself: "But God demonstrates his own love for us in this: While we were still sinners, Christ died for us." In that moment, Bud Paxon realized he was a sinner, but Christ had taken the judgment for his sin.

"The moment I put my faith in Jesus Christ and trusted him to forgive me, an overwhelming peace came over me. I knew at that moment God loved me. I knew he was with me."[5]

Bud Paxon met Jesus Christ in a Las Vegas hotel suite; Paul met the Savior on the road to Damascus. Both men's lives were forever changed after that moment of meeting.

After becoming a Christian, Paxon realized that he could touch thousands of lives through the power of television. In early 1991 he sold his interest in the Home Shopping Network and walked away with millions of dollars in his bank account—but what to do with all that money?

It didn't take long for him to realize that God had planted a dream in his heart. Why not create a twenty-four-hour worship television program? Paxon did not want the program to be a platform for preachers or a conduit to collect money. "Instead," he said,

> it would offer people hope by reminding them of God's presence and his love. Once God's dream captured me, I read every book I could find on the topic of worship, and within three weeks I had written a complete nonprofit business plan. The details of God's dream flowed from me like water from a pitcher.[6]

As a result of his experience with the Worship Network, he established PAX NET, a network with another specific purpose: to provide people with programs that will reinforce family values. Paxon says,

> I do not believe television is capable of developing a person spiritually. We can only plant the seed of faith through positive programming that communicates God's love and presence. A person needs Bible study, prayer, and fellowship in order to grow spiritually. The Bible makes it quite clear where growth occurs ... the Church.[7]

CO-LABORERS WITH CHRIST

The world is changing today, and God wants to use us to take the gospel to people wherever they are. Paxon had the background and contacts to do that through technology. The apostle Paul did not have modern technology to help him spread the gospel; he was limited to speaking in open-air meetings and crowded buildings. And sometimes he ministered one-on-one, as in the story of the Philippian jailer.

God asks that we make ourselves available to serve him. Let him give you a dream—a big dream—for service and ministry. Big dreams demand big motivations, and none are bigger or more beneficial than those that originate with our loving heavenly Father.

I smiled when a friend told me this story: A man fell asleep, and in a dream he heard the voice of God. "Come outside," God said, "I have something to show you."

So the man woke and went outside to find a huge boulder in his front lawn. "Now," God said, "push against the rock."

So the man pushed. And pushed. For days, weeks, and months he concentrated on pushing the boulder, but the big rock didn't budge.

Giving into discouragement, the man cried out to God. "I can't do it! You told me to push the boulder. I've tried with all my might, but it hasn't moved an inch!"

He heard a soft chuckle from above. "Why are you discouraged?" answered the Lord. "I told you to *push* the boulder—I never told you to *move* it. Only I can move a boulder of that size. But look at what has happened while you've been pushing—you've developed muscles, you've strengthened your patience, and tested your faith. So keep pushing until *I'm* ready to move the boulder."

I love that story. Though God will ultimately do the moving, he asks us to be co-laborers with him. He asks us to learn and stretch ourselves. He wants us to work as if everything depends on us, and pray as if everything depends upon him—because, ultimately, it does.

"The greatest dreams you can imagine will find their source in your greatest passions," says Bud Paxon.[8] What if your greatest dreams were bringing the Good News of Christ to the world? What surprises would be in store for you?

ten

SURPRISED BY
CONFLICT

DOES THE TITLE OF THIS CHAPTER SURPRISE YOU? ISN'T CONFLICT a bad thing? If so, why should we want God to surprise us with it?

Conflict is usually disagreeable; no one likes to argue with friends and family. We want other people to agree with us, and we can become irked—even angry—when they don't.

Though conflict can be uncomfortable, you must remember this: God is greater than annoyance, he is mightier than evil. And he can take anything and use it for his good.

In the previous chapter we learned about Paul's early years. Now let's look at the later part of his life, in the midst of his missionary journeys.

NO WAY, BARNABAS

Paul didn't travel alone. Like me in my year as Miss America, he traveled with a companion. His first partner in ministry was Barnabas, a kindred spirit. In the book of Acts, Luke calls Barnabas a "good man" (11:24). He was first on the list of prophets and teachers of the Antioch church.

We know Barnabas was Jewish, from the tribe of Levi, and a native of Cyprus, where he had been a landowner until he sold his land and turned to ministry. When Paul returned to Jerusalem after becoming a Christian, Barnabas took him under his wing and introduced him to the other disciples.

Paul and Barnabas may have known each other when they were studying to become rabbis. In any case, they traveled together for several years. The church at Jerusalem sent Barnabas to help the new church in Antioch. Once he arrived there and assessed the situation, "Barnabas went to Tarsus to look for Saul" (Acts 11:25), so they could work together as a team, staying there for a year. At one point they carried money from the wealthy Christians at Antioch to help poorer believers in Jerusalem, and there they met Barnabas's cousin, a young believer named John Mark. He returned with them to Antioch and worked with them in the church.

John Mark traveled with Paul and Barnabas on the first leg of an extended missionary trip to Cyprus and then into Asia Minor. At the end of that trip, back in Antioch, conflict arose between the two colleagues. Paul suggested that they start traveling again, revisiting the churches they had established around the Mediterranean. Barnabas wanted to take John Mark with them, but Paul did not think it wise to take him because he had deserted them in Pamphylia and had not continued with them in the work. They had such a sharp disagreement that they parted company. Barnabas took John Mark and sailed for Cyprus, and Paul chose Silas and left, commended by the brothers to the grace of the Lord (Acts 15:37–40).

Scripture gives us only a single clue as to what their disagreement was about. Acts 13:13 says that John Mark had lost heart and retreated from the work. Paul had lost respect for the young man; Barnabas wanted to give him a second chance. The two missionaries argued, and neither would give in. As a result, Paul and Barnabas went in separate directions.

If you're like me, you hate to argue with anyone. It's hard to believe two strong Christians like Barnabas and Paul could even *have* an argument. We want to think of the apostles as gentle, saintly creatures, but they were people of strong character and equally strong opinions.

Their disagreement was not pleasant and may even have been ugly. Perhaps they shouted at each other, or pouted, or stewed—they were human, after all. But even though their disagreement was not a good thing, good came out of it. Because of the division between them, *two* missionary teams traveled in that part of the world instead of one. John Mark got his second chance (and made good use of it), and Paul found an able companion in Silas.

The story has a pleasant postscript. When Paul was held prisoner in Rome at the end of his life, guess who he sent for? John Mark. "Only Luke is with me," Paul wrote to Timothy. "Get Mark and bring him with you, because he is helpful to me in my ministry" (2 Tim. 4:11).

In another letter, Paul wrote, "My fellow prisoner Aristarchus sends you his greetings, as does Mark, the cousin of Barnabas. (You have received instructions about him; if he comes to you, welcome him.)" (Col. 4:10)

So even though John Mark had been the source of a sharp disagreement between Paul and Barnabas, everything worked out. John Mark was probably with Paul at the end of his life, and his character had developed so much that he didn't retreat when the going got rough.

CONFLICTS CAN HELP IDENTIFY DREAMS

You may think you would be happier, healthier, and wealthier if you had no conflict in your life, but struggles shape and define us. We learn through conflict. We grow through testing. Sometimes conflict can help us identify what we really want—our true dreams. That became obvious to me in a conflict I had with John, early in our relationship.

The month after I surrendered my Miss America title and became Heather Whitestone, private citizen, I went to Washington, D.C., to speak at a meeting designed to acquaint our legislators with deaf issues. The organizers had gone through a lot of trouble to set up displays, organize the schedule, purchase billboards, and provide interpreters. I had worked hard on my speech and taken great care to look and sound professional in my delivery.

The organizers sent invitations to every senator and repre-
sentative, and I looked forward to speaking about the bene-
fits of an early hearing-loss detection program.

I was ready and eager to speak, but was sharply disappointed with the outcome. It seemed obvious that few
people in Washington cared enough to do more than put
in a token appearance. Some representatives came, stayed
five minutes, looked around, then left. One sent a staff
member to represent him. The vast majority never even
showed up. I lost most of the respect I held for politicians
in general, and considered it a waste of time to go through
the motions of speaking to Congress. None of the people
we were trying to reach were listening, and everyone at that
meeting knew it.

I was still unsettled, even furious, when I went to my
next engagement in North Carolina. When I had a free
moment, I called John, whom I had been steadily dating
when I could. "Look," I said. "I know you dream of serving in government. But ... those politicians ... well, they
stink. I don't know how you can serve God alongside
people like that. I don't think you should get involved in
politics at all."

When I paused from my tirade to catch a breath, I
heard dead silence on the phone. John wasn't sympathizing
with me. He wasn't saying anything. I felt a sudden wave
of crazy, erratic fear. Without even realizing it, I had given
him an ultimatum: your dream or me.

"If you can't support my dream," John said finally, his
voice flat and matter-of-fact, "then I can't see you anymore.

I don't want a woman—any woman—to take away the dream God has given me."

I didn't know what to do. I had been trying to imagine myself as his wife. But how could I be a politician's wife if I had no respect for politicians? I felt that most of them didn't respect other people's work. I had just seen evidence of that in Washington.

Still, was I honestly upset because they seemed not to care about deaf issues, or was I upset because they had slighted *me?*

Either way, I felt terrible. For a year as Miss America I had publicly touted the importance of following God-given dreams. John had confided in me about his dreams. Then, in a moment of fury, I had said, "Forget that dream. Those people hurt my feelings." Like a spoiled princess I had tried to control John; I had even tried to control God's plan for him.

That night I called John and apologized. As I spoke, I knew that God was calling me to marry him. In that conversation I also realized that a major disagreement can make or break a relationship. When I begged for John's forgiveness, he said he needed time to think things over.

Later that night, I prayed and asked God to forgive me too. My strong will and stubborn streak had reared its ugly head.

John and I didn't contact each other for several days. In that time of silence, I realized he was the man I needed, the man God had sent me. But I had to trust and I had to be patient. When John finally called me back to settle things between us, our love immediately deepened. With that one conflict as a catalyst, we moved from the foothills of friendship to the mountain of commitment. We identified our hope and dream of a lifetime together, as husband and wife.

COUNTERING THE STATUS QUO

Sometimes God introduces us to conflict that results from taking a stand for what we believe to be right. A good example is William Wilberforce, who was an elected member of the British Parliament when he committed his life to Christ in 1784, at the age of twenty-five. His new perspectives and changed motivations were not always popular with fellow politicians. In heated debates, he and his colleagues adamantly disagreed about dismantling Britain's slave trade.

As he worked to abolish slavery, Wilberforce sought advice from John Newton, a former slave trader who, after a dramatic Christian conversion, had changed careers. (We remember him best for writing the lyrics to "Amazing Grace.") As a respected pastor, Newton held strong opinions against slavery and encouraged the young politician to take up the controversial cause that had significant economic ramifications.

Early on, Wilberforce was optimistic about his campaign. But the much older Christian reformer John Wesley had a more realistic view. On his deathbed he wrote Wilberforce a letter saying, "Unless God has raised you up for this very thing, you will be worn out by the opposition of men and devils. But if God be for you who can be against you?"[1]

Wilberforce's twenty-year battle broke his health. He was physically assaulted. He received death threats. But he continued to make his reasoned argument against slavery, feeling that God had raised him up, like Daniel in Babylon and Joseph in Pharaoh's palace, to glorify God in the political arena.

In the heat of the verbal battles, a friend with a sense of humor wrote him saying, "I shall expect to read of you being carbonadoed by West Indian planters, barbecued by African merchants and eaten by Guinea captains, but do not be daunted, for—I will write your epitaph!"[2]

John Pollock, Wilberforce's biographer, says, "To face the onslaught Wilberforce needed all his Parliamentary skill, his patience, his sense of humor, his faith and prayer."[3]

Yes, Wilberforce was in the midst of conflict, but that doesn't mean he presented his case venomously. The poet Robert Southey described him by saying, "There is such a ... sweetness in all his tones, such a benignity in all his thoughts, words, and actions, that ... you can feel nothing but love and admiration for a creature of so happy and blessed a nature."[4]

In 1807, Wilberforce finally succeeded in orchestrating the passage of a bill that prohibited the buying and selling of slaves in Britain. The vote was overwhelming, 283 to 16. "In time," says Kevin Belmonte, a Wilberforce expert, "he helped many others to see that politics was a God-honoring calling, where the principles that are intrinsic to Christianity could again act as salt and light in a culture."[5]

Wilberforce hated conflict, but because he knew abolition was an important battle, he did not shy away from controversy. After a particularly heated skirmish in Parliament, he told his wife that he had found great consolation in Psalm 71. You can see why from this portion:

> My mouth is filled with your praise,
>> declaring your splendor all day long.
> Do not cast me away when I am old;
>> do not forsake me when my strength is gone.
> For my enemies speak against me;
>> those who wait to kill me conspire together.
> They say, "God has forsaken him;
>> pursue him and seize him,
>> for no one will rescue him."
> Be not far from me, O God;
>> come quickly, O my God, to help me.
> May my accusers perish in shame;
>> may those who want to harm me
>> be covered with scorn and disgrace.
> But as for me, I will always have hope;
>> I will praise you more and more.
> My mouth will tell of your righteousness,
>> of your salvation all day long,
>> though I know not its measure (Psalm 71:8–15).

Conflict, you see, is not always a bad thing. Sometimes we must endure conflict if we are to see change, for the enemies of Truth are everywhere and highly determined. If William Wilberforce had not accepted his holy calling in politics and pushed to eradicate the slave trade, who can say what would have happened in Britain? Perhaps they would have endured a terrible civil war. Or perhaps the human slave trade would have continued for several generations.

History has proved the worth of freedom and liberty. Wilberforce was right to press for abolition. Abraham Lincoln was right to give his efforts, and ultimately his life, to keep our country united.

And judging from the "end of the story" found in Scripture, Barnabas was right to give John Mark a second chance. Even so, if Paul and Barnabas had not disagreed, only one missionary team would have set out from Antioch, and half as many people would have heard about Jesus Christ. Because those people told other people, and those other people told more people still, it's fair to say that thousands of men and women accepted Jesus Christ because of one unresolved disagreement.

Sort of puts conflict in a positive light, doesn't it?

When conflict comes your way, pray about how you should resolve the situation, then do what the Spirit leads you to do. Do not worry or fret. God is in control, and what he does with your conflict may amaze you.

Don't despair when disagreements enter your life. Seek the counsel of wise and godly men and women. Check your motivations, stay true to God's word, and, if you discern it to be God's will, hold the course.

eleven

SURPRISED
BY ANGELS

WHEN I WAS ELEVEN YEARS OLD, MY PARENTS ENROLLED ME at a boarding school, Central Institute for the Deaf in St. Louis, Missouri. I loved CID and learned a lot there. One of my classmates, a girl from north Africa, told me a story I'll never forget. She said one night she had seen a beautiful angel in her bedroom.

I had never encountered an angel, but the idea of seeing one didn't frighten me at all. I had grown up in the Episcopal Church and knew about God, even though I couldn't follow the complicated service and found the King James Bible hard to understand. While the pastor talked, I usually made music in my heart or daydreamed about dancing to God's glory in the church.

But after hearing my friend's story, every night as I lay in the dorm at CID, I would envision myself dancing and watch for an angel. I believed God loved me, and I wouldn't have been at all surprised to see a heavenly guardian watching over me in the dorm.

Now that I have given my life to Christ, I know angels exist. I don't look for them every night, but I know they are there. They hover over me and my family, and they minister to us when we aren't even aware of their presence.

Scripture records many instances of people who encountered angels. At first sight, many were afraid. We already discussed Zechariah in the temple, before the birth of his son, John the Baptist: "Then an angel of the Lord appeared to him, standing at the right side of the altar of incense. When Zechariah saw him, he was startled and was gripped with fear" (Luke 1:11–12). But the angel delivered good news to Zechariah.

The shepherds in the Christmas story: "An angel of the Lord appeared to them, and the glory of the Lord shone around them, and they were terrified" (Luke 2:9). But the angel told them to fear not.

When thrown into the lions' den, Daniel claimed that he wasn't hurt: "My God sent his angel, and he shut the mouths of the lions" (Dan 6:22).

ANGELS 101

I was a little hesitant to include this chapter, because our society tends to make either too much or too little of angels. But I think it is important we realize their proper place in God's kingdom.

Quite simply, angels are messengers and servants of the most high God. (The word *angel* means "messenger.") They are not to be worshipped or adored, nor should we pray to them. Beware of anyone who emphasizes them more than the God they serve. The apostle Paul wrote, "Do not let anyone who delights in false humility and the worship of angels disqualify you for the prize. Such a person goes into great detail about what he has seen, and his unspiritual mind puffs him up with idle notions" (Col. 2:18).

Their actual appearances on earth are rare, but not as rare as you might think. "Do not forget to entertain strangers, for by so doing some people have entertained angels without knowing it" (Heb. 13:2).

The Bible tells us that angels were present in the beginning and shouted for joy at the creation of the world (Job 38:7). Like us, they are not creators but creations (Gen. 2:1, Neh. 9:6, Col. 1:16); yet as creations, they are not human. I have heard people say things like "She's dead now, but she's an angel in heaven," and that's just not true. People are people; they will never be angels.

Angels do not marry (Matt. 22:30), they are obedient (Ps. 103:20), and they are concerned about earthly affairs. With all the recent interest in prophecy, it's refreshing to know that even the angels are incredibly interested in the last days (1 Peter 1:12).

As impressive as angels are, remember that we will one day judge the angels who chose to disobey God. Paul wrote, "Do you not know that we will judge angels?" (1 Cor. 6:3). Scripture indicates that before God created the world, many angels chose to side with Lucifer in his war with God. Lucifer's angels were cast out of heaven along with him: "And the angels who did not keep their positions of authority but abandoned their own home—these he has kept in darkness, bound with everlasting chains for judgment on the great Day" (Jude 1:6, see also Job 4:18, Matt. 25:41, 2 Peter 2:4, Rev. 12:9). These are the angels we will one day judge.

Angels number in the millions, and they are organized in ranks with specialized tasks, much like our armed forces. Though they can appear to be clothed in flesh (Abraham ate and drank with three angels who visited him), they are spirit beings. They are immortal and possess superhuman might and power. Yet angels are not omnipresent or omniscient. They live to serve God and his people. They protect us, they minister to us, and they rejoice every time a sinner repents and turns to God (Luke 15:10). They are equally at home serving Christians in the public eye as they are ministering to children and invalids. We should be humbled when we realize that millions of angels serve God by serving us!

Much of their ministry goes unseen, yet we benefit from it every day of our lives. They do battle for us against the spiritual forces of darkness, and they comfort us when we need a touch of grace.

ANGELS OF PROTECTION

When researching one of her novels, my cowriter, Angela Hunt, ran across a fascinating account of angels in a book about South American Indians. In his book *Spirit of the Rainforest,* Mark Andrew Ritchie relates the true story of a shaman from a tribe in the Amazon River basin that had experienced only limited contact with the civilized world. I especially like this story because it comes from people who have not grown up in church or heard stories of angels.

This tribe, the Yanomamo, lived in several villages. The Honey Village had accepted the teachings of the missionaries and prayed to God, whom they called Yai Pada. Another settlement, Mouth Village, was angry with Honey Village and threatened to attack.

All night long Spear, one of the Honey warriors, worried—and prayed—about the coming attack. Then at dawn,

> as he stepped from his house onto the wet grass, he saw that Honey Village was surrounded by people, warriors maybe; he wasn't sure. But there were so many of them, big beautiful people in bright white shirts that went down to their feet. Spear could tell that Yai Pada had sent them to protect Honey from all the attacks. But after the sun came up, they were gone. And no one in the village had seen them. He asked Pepe if Yai Pada had people like that. Pepe said, "I've never seen them, but his book says that he has them and they can protect you."[1]

This story reminds me of the time the prophet Elisha and his servant were living in Dothan, a small town near Samaria. For some time, the Spirit of God had been giving Elisha advance warning of Aram's ambushes. Elisha in turn warned the king of Israel, and as a result the king of Israel had avoided every attack.

Frustrated and furious, the king of Aram sent spies to discover where Elisha was living. In the dead of night, the king sent chariots and warriors to surround Dothan. Early that morning Elisha's servant went out to check out the scenery. He came back in the house with alarming news: "An army with horses and chariots had surrounded the city. 'Oh, my lord, what shall we do?' the servant asked" (2 Kings 6:15).

Elisha went outside, saw the same amassed army—but more. He calmly told his servant not to be afraid. "'Those who are with us are more than those who are with them.' Elisha then prayed, 'O Lord, open his eyes so he may see.' Then the Lord opened the servant's eyes, and he looked and saw the hills full of horses and chariots of fire all around Elisha" (2 Kings 6:16–17).

In her book *Heaven,* Joni Eareckson Tada comments, "What was true for Elisha is true for any believer. When we sing at church, 'Open my eyes that I may see / Glimpses of truth Thou hast for me,' we wouldn't believe our eyes if God answered our request. Our eyes would pop at all the hosts of angels."[2]

ESCORTS FOR GOD'S CHILDREN

One of my favorite TV shows is *Touched by an Angel.* Although I don't agree with every human aspect they assign to angels, I do love the way they portray angels ministering to people. I especially love the depiction of how an angel escorts children of God to heaven at the moment of death.

The assurance that we are attended by angels at death comes from a parable Jesus told. In the story, a beggar dies and angels carry him to Abraham's side (Luke 16:22). And though I am lifting the next verse out of context, I believe the principle is still evident. In Exodus 23:20, God assured the children of Israel that he would be with them through the wilderness journey and bring them to a place of safety in the promised land: "See, I am sending an angel ahead of you to guard you along the way and to bring you to the place I have prepared."

Doesn't the same principle apply to us who will wander through life's wilderness while seeking the place our Lord Jesus has prepared? I firmly believe that angels will serve as our escorts as we leave our tired physical bodies and journey to the place where Jesus waits to welcome us home. After all, Paul assures us that to be "away from the body" is to be "at home with the Lord" (2 Cor. 5:8).

You are probably familiar with Joni Eareckson Tada's story: As a seventeen-year-old, she broke her neck in a diving accident in the Chesapeake Bay. For more than thirty years, Joni has been a quadriplegic. She has written a whole book about heaven, anticipating the time when she will be at home with her Lord and free of the constriction of her paralyzed body. In that book she includes a startling but comforting night scene:

> It was 2:00 A.M. on a pitch-black night. I was wide
> awake, propped up in bed, and straining my ears
> to hear the muffled voices of my family in the bed-
> room directly above me. They were surrounding

the bed of my five-year-old niece, Kelly, who was dying of cancer. We knew her passing into heaven could happen at any moment, but I was unable to get up the narrow stairs to say good-bye with the others. Suddenly, a brilliant golden shape that glowed whisked by the large bay window I was facing—it didn't move from left to right, but from bottom to top. I screamed. I then searched to see if there were cars on the street outside. Nothing was there. In the next second, my sister Jay called down the steps, "Kelly's gone!"

A few of the family came downstairs to find out why I screamed. I told them exactly what I saw. My sisters sank on the edge of my bed in amazement. We knew I had seen a large spiritual being, probably sent from heaven to escort Kelly's soul into eternity.[3]

In the *Spirit of the Rainforest,* Mark Andrew Ritchie tells another Yanomamo story, about Redhair, from Honey Village, who lay near death, having been severely beaten by warriors from Forgetful Village. The village elders convened in his presence to discuss whether they should take revenge.

Suddenly Redhair sat up, claimed he felt "just fine," and told them to listen up.

"Like so many of you, I'm a child of Yai Pada, the great spirit. Now, as you can see all around you," he said, pointing around the house, "his people have come here to take me home. So I'm going with them now, and I just want to say before I go that I don't want any of you to even think about taking revenge against Forgetful Village."[4]

The elders took issue with him:

> "There's no one here to take you," they said, look-
> ing around. "You're well. You're going to be fine."
>
> Redhair was shocked. "Can't you see these
> people?" he asked. "They're standing all around
> here, waiting for me to finish talking to you."
> Everyone stared at him and shook their heads. "I
> can't believe you can't see them! Look, right
> there," he said, pointing to places around the
> house. No one saw anything . . .
>
> "Well, they're here for me and I'm going with
> them to Yai Pada. We won't need revenge where
> I'm going, so please don't take any on Forgetful
> Village."
>
> For the first time a crowd of Yanomamo had
> nothing to say. They watched quietly as Redhair
> lay back down on his hammock, curled up and
> died.[5]

I believe that God filled Redhair's house with angelic
escorts. Until that time, villagers had lived by the laws of
war and revenge. But his death and plea to refrain from
revenge taught the Yanomamo a great lesson about loving
one's enemies.

E L I S H A ' S S T O R Y , C H A P T E R T W O

Think back to the story of Elisha and his servant. The
king of Aram had surrounded the city of Dothan with
chariots and armed warriors. The morning sun glinted off
weapons, the bridles of snorting horses, and the drawn
brows of men already perspiring beneath their armor. Their

eyes were narrowed, their jaws set. They were waiting for the sun to light the city, then they would attack the sleepy inhabitants and do whatever it took to kill Elisha and anyone else who happened to be in the vicinity.

No wonder Elisha's servant was so frightened. Wailing in fear, he ran to the prophet: "Master, look outside! We are surrounded!"

But Elisha, who had already looked out upon the scene with *spiritual* eyes, knew they were not alone. He saw the soldiers of heaven around the city walls. These angelic warriors faced the army of Aram, ready to defend God's prophet against his attackers.

Sensing the power of God at hand, Elisha made a bold and unusual prayer request. As the warriors of Aram came toward him, Elisha asked God to strike them with physical blindness. God answered that prayer, and then Elisha and his servant strode out to meet the blind and confused army.

> "Follow me, and I will lead you to the man you are looking for." And he led them to Samaria.
>
> After they entered the city, Elisha said, "Lord, open the eyes of these men so they can see." Then the Lord opened their eyes and they looked, and there they were, inside Samaria (2 Kings 6:19–20).

Samaria, you see, happened to be the city where the king of Israel was headquartered—with his army. So Elisha walked the king's enemies straight into Israel's command post, then said, "Surprise! Guess where you are?!"

Can you imagine how horrified—and terrified—Aram's men must have been? Even the king of Israel was startled; he hadn't expected his enemies to appear at his breakfast table!

> When the king of Israel saw them, he asked Elisha, "Shall I kill them, my father? Shall I kill them?"
>
> "Do not kill them," he answered. "Would you kill men you have captured with your own sword or bow? Set food and water before them so that they may eat and drink and then go back to their master." So he prepared a great feast for them, and after they had finished eating and drinking, he sent them away, and they returned to their master. So the bands from Aram stopped raiding Israel's territory (2 Kings 6:21–23).

Elisha advised the king of Israel to repay evil with mercy—the same advice Redhair gave to the warriors of Honey Village. And in both situations, the appearance of angels gave men of God the courage to lead their people from war to peace.

BLESSED SPECTATORS

Henry Ward Beecher wrote, "We not only live among men, but there are airy hosts, blessed spectators, sympathetic lookers-on, that see and know and appreciate our thoughts and feelings and acts."[6]

Would it encourage you to know that scores of unseen beings are watching and cheering you on as you struggle through difficult situations? Sometimes we feel lonely, yet we are never alone. The Holy Spirit of God resides within every believer in Christ, and angels stand by to minister to us. Furthermore, our loved ones in heaven look down upon us. I believe they are watching to encourage us.

I find great encouragement in the heavenly hint given to us in Hebrews 12:1: "Since we are surrounded by such a great cloud of witnesses, let us throw off everything that hinders and the sin that so easily entangles, and let us run with perseverance the race marked out for us."

The next time I am tempted to lose my temper, become depressed, or say something I shouldn't, I can always remember that I'm not alone. The Lord is watching and listening and so are myriad angels, not to mention certain believers who may be watching from the balconies of heaven. It is easier to behave when you know you're standing before an invisible audience!

ANGELS AT HAND

I have never seen an angel, but I know they have worked overtime in my life. They protected me in childhood and through my teenage years, and I'm convinced they helped me during the Miss America pageant.

My talent for the Miss America competition was a ballet set to Sandy Patty's recording of "Via Dolorosa." Near the end of that song, I had to do a series of rapid turns. It is a difficult progression; a dancer must imagine herself to be a playing card so that her entire body turns all at once. If I moved my head before my body, or vice versa, I would lose my balance.

I tended to make mistakes in that tricky section; in fact, during the preliminary talent competition I hadn't turned properly. I had lost my balance and nearly tumbled over a step at the back of the performing area.

But on the night I danced for America, God told me to relax. When I came to that series of turns, I could have sworn that an angel was pushing my shoulder forward, providing the momentum I needed to remain straight and keep going. I just stood there and spun. I have never felt anything quite like that before or since. My dance was timed to be two minutes and thirty seconds, but that night I thought someone had hurried the tape. I danced for what felt like half a minute at most. I sensed that one of God's ministering angels had hovered near to boost my confidence and guide my body.

You may never see an angel on earth, but I am sure you'll see thousands of them as soon as you approach heaven. Until then, know that you can place your life in the strong hands of a God who loves you enough to send supernatural servants to guard you, protect you, and minister to your heart and soul.

Let God surprise you—through the ministry of his angels.

twelve

SURPRISED
BY BEAUTY

∽

A PERSIAN PALACE PARTY

When I was young, I loved hearing the Old Testament story of brave Queen Esther. I didn't know much about her life, but in Sunday school my teacher led us to believe she entered a contest and won a throne and king!

When I grew old enough to read the Bible story for myself, I glossed over details. But one fact jumped out at me: Esther was exceptionally beautiful, "lovely in form and features" (Esther 2:7).

Before I knew better, I assumed that Esther had willingly entered some sort of national beauty pageant, trained for over a year to perfect her talent and focus her style, then wept with delight when the king placed a crown upon her head. Upon closer study, I realized that I had been reading the story of Esther through rose-colored glasses.

Let's look at the biblical account more closely. Esther, whose Hebrew name was Hadassah, was an orphan who had been adopted by her cousin, an upstanding and wise man called Mordecai. They lived in Susa, capital of the Persian Empire ruled by King Xerxes, whom the Hebrews called Ahasuerus.

Ahasuerus's empire stretched from India to eastern Africa. In the prime of life, he was militarily strong and incredibly wealthy. In his third year as king, he threw a state dinner that lasted six full *months;* the guest list included military officers, noblemen, and officials from all 127 Persian provinces.

Ahasuerus wanted to throw a party, yes. But he also wanted to show off, perhaps even engage in a little intimidation. With every display of wealth and strength, he would be saying: *Think twice before you rise up against me.*

His gargantuan banquet was a tremendous success. When it was over, Ahasuerus felt generous toward the local people who had worked hard to put the event together. As a grand thank-you gesture, he hosted a smaller banquet for all the palace servants and officials, inviting everyone from the prime minister to the boy who fanned the flies from royal horses at the stable. He held the sumptuous banquet in the garden of his own palace. In a detailed description of the banquet, Scripture says, "the royal wine was abundant, in keeping with the king's liberality" (Esther 1:7).

Everything was proceeding smoothly—until the last day, when the king ordered his queen, Vashti, to parade in front of his guests. He wanted to "display her beauty to the people and nobles, for she was lovely to look at. But when the attendants delivered the king's command, Queen Vashti refused to come. Then the king became furious and burned with anger" (Esther 1:11–12).

No one knows why Vashti refused the king's order. The Bible says she was holding a feast for the women at the same time the king honored the men, but apparently the king expected her to drop everything to obey his bidding.

Some scholars believe Vashti deserves our praise. We do know the king was "in high spirits from the wine." Vashti might have been acting out of courage rather than stubbornness. I know I wouldn't want to get all dressed up and stand before a group of drunken men so they could ogle me. Remember, these were the palace staff, the men who served Vashti and Ahasuerus every day. The king wanted her to come and parade before the men; he fully intended to give his inebriated guests a "treat" by displaying a beautiful woman. His unspoken message: *She is just another of my many treasures.*

The king's attitude wouldn't have been unusual for that day and age. Women were little more than chattel in many cultures, even women who were queens. Whatever her motivation, Vashti refused to obey the king's command. Her unspoken message: *I am not a possession you can display before your drunken friends.*

What's a king to do when his wife rebels? Well, this king boiled with anger. I imagine he dismissed the feast in an uproar. Then he called legal advisors and asked, "What

can I legally do to a queen who disobeys a proper order?"
After the advisors huddled together, one of them gave a
recommendation along with a rationale:

> "Queen Vashti has done wrong, not only against the
> king but also against all the nobles and the peoples
> of all the provinces of King Xerxes. For the queen's
> conduct will become known to all the women, and
> so they will despise their husbands and say, 'King
> Xerxes commanded Queen Vashti to be brought
> before him, but she would not come.' This very day
> the Persian and Median women of the nobility who
> have heard about the queen's conduct will respond
> to all the king's nobles in the same way. There will
> be no end of disrespect and discord.
>
> "Therefore, if it pleases the king, let him issue a
> royal decree and let it be written in the laws of
> Persia and Media, which cannot be repealed, that
> Vashti is never again to enter the presence of King
> Xerxes. Also let the king give her royal position to
> someone else who is better than she. Then when the
> king's edict is proclaimed throughout all his vast
> realm, all the women will respect their husbands,
> from the least to the greatest" (Esther 1:16–20).

The king's men wasted no time putting a lid on that can
of worms! Lest all the women of the kingdom rise up to
disobey their husbands, Ahasuerus decreed that Vashti be
sent into exile and another woman be found to take her
place. The king and his men hurried to publish the decision; letters were written and sent throughout the empire:
Husbands were to be lords in their own households; wives
were to obey.

After Ahasuerus's anger cooled, his men turned to the task of finding him a new queen. They proposed an empire-wide search "for beautiful young virgins" for the king's harem. "Under the care of Hegai, the king's eunuch . . . let beauty treatments be given to them. Then let the girl who pleases the king be queen instead of Vashti" (Esther 2:2–4). This advice appealed to the king, and he followed it.

The king's personal assistants were clever. They knew the kingdom abounded with beautiful women. Surely the king could find one with the charm, wit, and intelligence he required in a queen!

On the surface, the king's search for a queen sounds romantic and glamorous. Viewing through rose-colored glasses, you might imagine the king's men riding out on white horses, pausing beside beautiful women to gallantly kneel and present them with engraved invitations to visit the king. These beautiful girls would twitter and blush and stammer, then happily leap onto the backs of the white steeds and gallop away to the palace, where they would be treated to perfumed baths and professional stylists.

Nothing could be further from the truth. Remember, women were little more than possessions in Persian society. We have already seen that the king—along with almost every man in the kingdom—was determined to rule women with a strong hand.

I don't think the king's search parties enlisted any polished knights riding white horses. I imagine he sent cage-like war wagons manned by burly, unshaven soldiers who went from village to village seeking pretty girls. Because many women veiled themselves in those days, in my mind's eye I see the king's men ripping the veils from women's heads, lifting their skirts to evaluate their form, peering in their mouths to check their teeth. Girls deemed too ugly were rudely cast aside; pretty girls were forced into the rough wagons where other young women wept and wailed.

The king's men sought virgins. And because women married soon after beginning menstruation, the king's men probably sought out girls who were hardly teens. Onward rolled the king's wagons, disrupting families throughout the empire of Persia. Young girls were taken from their parents, their betrothed husbands, their siblings. This was more like mass kidnapping than a beauty pageant. When the experience was over, the contestants who didn't win weren't allowed to go home with happy memories and a consolation prize. Once they were taken into the king's possession, they became his personal property. Forever.

Hadassah was one of those captured young women. The orphan reared by her beloved cousin Mordecai had been raised in the Jewish faith. Like other Hebrew girls, she had been taught to pray to the one true God, to revere him, to wait for the coming Messiah.

And now she had been stolen by a pagan king. I don't know what dreams Hadassah cherished in her heart, but I imagine she dreamed of a wedding and a husband and children—perhaps even of being the mother of the Messiah. But as soon as she was snatched by the king's men, all those dreams crumbled to ashes

Warned by her guardian cousin not to speak of her nationality, she "was taken to the king's palace" (Esther

2:8). I'm sure her legs trembled as she walked from the dusty road into the palace enclosure. Her heart must have pounded as she looked at a sea of female faces from across the empire—girls who would become her new family. For unless God intervened, she would never see Mordecai again.

How could God use her in a pagan king's palace? Why had she bothered to be faithful and observant if she had been ordained to spend her life as a concubine in a *harem?*

But in the king's palace, Scripture says, she won the favor of Hegai, the eunuch in charge. He gave her the standard beauty treatment—six months of oil of myrrh followed by six months with special perfumes and ointments. She was sheltered from the sun to protect her skin; she was taught to dance, to walk, to smile in a way the king found appealing. But she was also given "the best place in the harem"; there was obviously something about her that struck Hegai as special.

After the year of pampered preparation, the young women lived in the House of the Virgins until the king called for a woman. When Hegai received a summons, he chose a girl from among his charges. To impress the king she was allowed to select whatever garments and jewelry she wanted. After sleeping with him, she went to live in the House of the Wives, never to visit the king again unless he remembered her and called for her by name.

Hadassah, now called by the Persian name "Esther," meaning "star," must have been lonely as she endured the year of beauty rituals. When Hegai deemed her ready, he asked what she wanted to wear. Apparently having learned to trust Hegai's judgment, Esther left the choice up to him. Dressed to his satisfaction, she walked before the other women, and everyone agreed that she looked extraordinary. She "won the favor of everyone who saw her" (Esther 2:15).

That night Esther pleased the king. He was "attracted to Esther more than to any of the other women, and she won his favor and approval more than any of the other virgins" (2:17). Satisfied that his search was over, "he set a royal crown on her head and made her queen instead of Vashti" (2:17). He gave a great banquet and proclaimed a holiday in her honor. Something tells me that Esther respected Ahasuerus, for she took pains to please and honor him.

FINDING PURPOSE IN A GILDED PRISON

We'll fast forward a few scenes. Unknown to Esther, one of the king's top advisors, Haman, grew to hate Esther's cousin Mordecai. In a grand scheme to strike at the Jews, Haman convinced the king that the Jews were troublemaking insurgents and should be eradicated. With no reason to doubt Haman's word, Ahasuerus signed an edict allowing anyone in his kingdom to kill Jews on—a roll of the dice produced the date—March 7, 473 B.C.

The Jews were horrified, and Mordecai risked his life getting word to Esther. "You must go to the king," he told her.

> Do not think that because you are in the king's house you alone of all the Jews will escape. For if you remain silent at this time, relief and deliverance for the Jews will arise from another place, but you and your father's family will perish. And who

knows but that you have come to royal position
for such a time as this? (Esther 4:13–14)

Stunned and saddened, Esther faced the hard facts:
Vashti had been exiled for refusing to go to the king when
called; Esther could face the same fate, or worse, for doing
the opposite—visiting the king when he had *not* called. Persian law expressly stated that anyone who approached the
king without permission would summarily be killed unless
the king held out his scepter in pardon.

Esther probably thought a lot about the former queen
as she debated her options. Vashti had been beautiful too,
and a woman of courage, and yet the king had still exiled
her. And who knew if Ahasuerus would stop at exile for
the second queen to defy his order? He might choose to kill
Esther.

Gathering her courage, Esther sent a message to Mordecai, asking the Jewish people to join her in a three-day fast.
"When this is done, I will go to the king, even though it is
against the law. And if I perish, I perish" (Esther 4:16).

I can only imagine what Esther was thinking during
those three days of fasting and prayer. Her childhood
dreams had crumbled, but in their place she had built a
happy life. She liked the king, perhaps she even loved him,
and he had loved her enough to make her his queen. But,
Esther admitted to Mordecai, the king had not sent for her
in over a month. Had he lost interest? Was he spending his
nights with other women from the harem? Had he a new
favorite, or was he distressed by other thoughts? Perhaps he
had already learned of her heritage and determined that she

should die, since he had demonstrated no reluctance to sign Haman's proclamation against the Jews.

Esther didn't know what her husband was thinking, and royal protocol kept the king at arms' length. If she went to him, she had no way of knowing if she would be welcomed with love or hate.

Three days after sending her message to Mordecai, Esther dressed in her royal robes and entered the inner court of the palace. Jaws dropped as she approached, for no one had heard the king send for her. Besides, wives belonged in the bed chamber, not in the royal audience hall! What would Ahasuerus say if she strode in to see him?

In a bold voice Esther barely recognized as her own, she commanded the guards to open the doors. Every head in the main hall must have turned as the huge doors swung open, every eye must have bulged as Queen Esther walked through the center of the assembled throng.

Who knows what thoughts ran through Ahasuerus's mind? But something in Esther's appearance touched his heart. "When he saw Queen Esther standing in the court, he was pleased with her and held out to her the gold scepter that was in his hand" (5:2). That gesture spared her life. "What is it, Queen Esther? What is your request? Even up to half the kingdom, it will be given you" (5:3).

With great poise and confidence, Esther simply invited him to a banquet that evening. I'll be there, he said, and at the dinner he repeated his offer: "Tell me what you want; I'll give up to half my kingdom." She smiled and invited him to a second banquet. And that's where she exposed Haman's plan to exterminate her people.

By dawn Haman was hanged—on the very gallows he had built for the purpose of executing Mordecai. In short order Esther and Mordecai became the king's best advisors, helping him devise a plan to save the Jewish people. Though the king could not rescind the order to attack Esther's people on March 7, a subsequent edict gave them the right to defend themselves and fight back.

Esther's courage, confidence, and devotion to her people saved thousands of lives. Although the name of God does not appear anywhere in this book of the Bible, it is clear that the Almighty was orchestrating events in Esther's life. Of the book of Esther, one theologian said, "Though the name of God be not in it, his finger is."

Esther was so much more than a pretty girl—she was a woman of deep faith, courage, and thoughtful caution. She was a loyal daughter to Mordecai, a faithful wife to Ahasuerus, a brave member of the Jewish people.

DON'T IGNORE WISE COUNSEL

Esther had Mordecai to speak truth to her—I have always had my family. They are the people who know me best, and believe me, there are no stars in their eyes when they look at me. To them, I'm just Heather, as I'm sure Esther was simply "Hadassah" to Mordecai.

When I first began to compete in local pageants, I failed to win because I pretended to be a hearing girl. I had terrible interviews because many times the judges were looking down at their papers while asking me questions, so I couldn't read their lips. I didn't want them to know about my problems with deafness, so I just pressed on, guessing what they had said.

You can imagine what a disaster those interviews were. After my family watched the videotape of my interviews, they said the problem was *me,* not my deafness. I was too proud to admit I needed help—if I could fix that, I would do better.

So the next time I competed, I explained my deafness to the judges and asked them to look at me when they spoke so I could read their lips. They were very helpful, and I won that pageant. But my first pageant, the one I lost, taught me the most. That's where I learned how to improve.

There have been other times when my family spoke truth to me—and sometimes I didn't want to hear it. But ultimately, I know they love me and want only what is best for me. Having a support system—whether it is family or friends or fellow believers—does much to instill confidence in a woman. And confidence does much to make a woman beautiful and attractive.

True beauty is so much more than physical appearance. Although physical beauty is valued by men and can be used of God, it is not a quality the Lord seeks in his children. He wants us to be beautiful on the *inside,* "the unfading beauty of a gentle and quiet spirit, which is of great worth in God's sight" (1 Peter 3:4).

"But I don't feel confident!" you may say. "And the people in my life seem more intent on tearing me down than building me up!"

If this situation describes you, let's look at Proverbs 22:11: "He who loves a pure heart and whose speech is gracious will have the king for his friend."

Do you want to share the confidence of Esther and Vashti? Would you like to feel as confident as a Miss America when you enter a crowded room? There are clues in this verse that will help you: first, love a pure heart. Don't let your heart and mind be cluttered by the glittering images the world sets before our eyes. Don't yearn for looks and symbols and things that have more to do with worldly pride than eternal value.

Second, cultivate gracious speech. Don't gossip about your friends and neighbors. Don't rush to spread the rumor you have just heard. Don't criticize, condemn, or crush others with hurtful comments.

If you will learn to look upon others with discernment, and if you will train your tongue to speak with love instead of bitterness, the Bible says you will become someone VIPs would like to have over for dinner. Well, that's a loose paraphrase, but I hope you get my point!

BEAUTIFUL BENEFITS

As a former Miss America, I am often asked about my beauty regime, but I really don't obsess over beauty or style. I would much rather concentrate on developing a beautiful spirit, a tender heart, and a wise mind. Best of all, as I seek those qualities, in the eyes of God I will grow more beautiful each day! I will become more and more like Jesus, the fairest of the fair.

I do try to keep in shape; I think my ballet training helps this come naturally. Exercise is important to me because God blessed me with my body and I must take good care of it. I want to feel good about myself so I will earn other people's respect. Being in good shape helps me to maintain a healthy level of self-esteem.

But about personal beauty—people often tell me that I am more beautiful in person than in my photographs or on television. I am flattered by the compliment, but I know they are saying that because when people see my face and figure in a picture, they are only seeing the outer shell. When they meet me, I think they catch a glimpse of Jesus inside me, and he is the most beautiful person in all the universe. If I am beautiful in person, it's because Jesus lights my eyes and sparks my smile. He is the gracefulness of my hands, the spring in my step, the lightness of my legs. The Bible says:

> How beautiful on the mountains
>   are the feet of those who bring good news,
> who proclaim peace,
>   who bring good tidings,
>   who proclaim salvation,
> who say to Zion,
>   "Your God reigns!" (Isaiah 52:7)

I love that verse—even my battered ballet feet are beautiful when I'm dancing for God's glory!

I always read in the Bible about how important our heart is to God, and I believe that beauty from the heart is what brings glory to God. When I hear people talk about how beautiful I am, I often feel embarrassed. I want to be more beautiful on the inside than on the outside. Sometimes I wish I were more kind and gentle and giving—that's real beauty.

Last Sunday I was planting pansies in our backyard garden and my husband, John, took a few moments to tell me that I was beautiful in his eyes. He was proud of me because I worked hard to lose the thirty-five pounds I had gained in my two pregnancies.

His words meant more to me than compliments from the president of the United States. I want to please my husband because I believe marriage is important to God. Sitting there in the garden, sprinkled with dirt and surrounded by empty plastic containers, I was a long way from cover girl beautiful—but I have never felt more loved and cherished.

As the story of Esther demonstrates, the world is filled with beautiful women, but women who are filled with courage, faith, and devotion will rise above the rest. You can be an Esther too. Even when you feel your dreams have crumbled to dust, you can turn to the God who made you and loves you, and trust him to bring you up from the ashes clothed in honor, confidence, and glory.

Let God surprise you with beauty—where you least expect it.

thirteen

SURPRISED BY HEALING

One afternoon some people brought to Jesus a man who was deaf and could hardly talk, which tells me he probably lost his hearing in his early childhood. Having heard about Jesus' healing miracles, they begged Jesus to touch and heal the deaf man.

> After he took him aside, away from the crowd, Jesus put his fingers into the man's ears. Then he spit and touched the man's tongue. He looked up to heaven and with a deep sigh said to him, "Ephphatha!" (which means "Be opened!"). At this, the man's ears were opened, his tongue was loosened and he began to speak plainly.
>
> Jesus commanded them not to tell anyone. But the more he did so, the more they kept talking

about it. People were overwhelmed with amaze-
ment. "He has done everything well," they said.
"He even makes the deaf hear and the mute speak"
(Mark 7:33–37).

Notice Jesus' personal care for this deaf man. This
wasn't an instantaneous healing where Jesus healed by a
mere word—instead, he drew the man aside, away from
the crowd, he touched him with tenderness, and he placed
his hands upon the affected parts of the man's face—his
ears and his tongue. And then the man demonstrated that
he could not only hear, but he could speak clearly!

MEETING MY SON'S NEED

If you have been given the gift of hearing, I'm not sure
you can understand what it is like to live in a silent world.
You may think you are sitting in a quiet room, but if you
stop and listen carefully, I understand you'll hear the hum
of fluorescent lights, the quiet roar of a fan, the shush of
passing cars on the street. Even if you live in a rural envi-
ronment, your quiet can be punctuated by the breath of
wind through the trees, the creak of settling timber in a
house, and muffled birdsongs outside your window. I have
read about these sounds in books, but even with my hearing aid, I missed most of them.

Deafness is silence, deep and intense. Those of us who
hear with a hearing aid hear only selected sounds, and the
level of those sounds does not approach what you hear.

Have you ever videotaped someone outside and then
watched the tape—and were amazed that the chirping of

some bird you didn't even notice is practically drowning out the voice of the person you videotaped? The same sort of thing happens with a hearing aid. In a crowded banquet room, sometimes the clink of silverware and glasses drowns out the voices of the people sitting across from me.

Still, after wearing a hearing aid for twenty-seven years, I have adjusted. I have learned to read lips, to speak, and to sign, though I prefer to read lips whenever possible. And yes, I suppose I have grown used to silence.

I have also realized that deafness was part of God's plan for me. In Exodus 4:11 we read, "Who gave man his mouth? Who makes him deaf or mute? Who gives him sight or makes him blind? Is it not I, the Lord?"

If I had grown up with my hearing, I don't know that I would have entered pageants or won the Miss America title. I know I would not have had a platform to represent deaf people across this nation. If I had not been Miss America, I would not have met my husband and met the many people who have influenced my life in so many ways.

God had a plan for me.

I was satisfied with my hearing aid for many years. With it, I was able to hear some sounds in my left ear— sirens, thunder, music, and the telephone. I could also hear the high pitches of the oven timer and the seatbelt reminder in my car. But I couldn't listen to radio talk shows, and I depended heavily on close-captioning for TV programs.

I'm so grateful I had a hearing aid. For me, it opened the doors to dance and music and so many conversations. Yet I have special reasons to be grateful for technology God has motivated Christian men to develop.

One beautiful day in November 2001, we opened our French doors so our son, little John, could play outside on the patio. I watched from inside the house. A few minutes later, however, I saw my husband run toward little John because he had fallen and was crying.

The fact that I could not hear my son crying—even with my hearing aid—bothered me a great deal. All my life, I have always thought I heard well enough to deal with the hearing world. But I hadn't heard John crying.

This wasn't the first time I as a mother had missed something. How many times had family members told me what my boys had said behind me, where I couldn't see their lips? Babysitters and family members got so excited when my boys said their first words, but I had to hear the news secondhand. At other times the boys would point at something and ask me what certain sounds meant. My heart sank because I could not answer their questions.

As I thought about it, I became concerned. As my boys grew older, how could I know if they were listening to inappropriate music or vulgar talk shows if I couldn't hear? I knew I would feel incredibly left out if I missed out on their conversations, school plays, and concerts.

Soon after little John's accident on the patio, I stood in front of my kitchen window and begged God to give me more hearing. Almost immediately, he turned my thoughts toward a cochlear implant.

You may not have heard of a cochlear implant, but the surgical procedure is becoming more common. The so-called "bionic ear" is a highly technical medical device that electrically stimulates the inner ear and allows deaf individuals to hear sound. More than 20,000 profoundly deaf people in fifty-five countries have received hearing through cochlear implants.

Since winning the Miss America title, I have been asked many times about my interest in the procedure. I always replied that I was satisfied to live in the hearing world with only the help of my hearing aid. But my boys have taught me a lot about my deafness. I have been missing far more sounds than I realized.

GOD'S MIRACLE?

When I began to research the possibility of having a cochlear implant in my right ear (which does not benefit from a hearing aid), I wasn't crazy about the idea of having surgery. I was hoping God would heal my deafness through some sort of medical miracle.

I was still uncertain about having the surgery until I read *Sounds from Silence: Graeme Clark and the Bionic Ear Story*. Dr. Clark performed the first successful cochlear implant and has been working on improving the procedure for thirty years. Clark's father was deaf, so there is no doubt God used that situation to plant a dream within Clark's heart—to help deaf people. He became a Christian while in college and grew in faith as he studied the Bible.

Years later, God blessed Clark with the opportunity to implement his vision of a cochlear implant. Research wasn't as easy as he thought it was going to be. The first six animals he used for the experimental surgery died on the operating table from toxic materials in the anesthetic. Added to this dilemma were his troubles with funding and materials. Not many people believed in his dream, so not many were willing to contribute.

When he performed his first surgery upon a human ear, Dr. Clark felt God's hand directing him. The operation was a success. His deaf client gained hearing capability. Dr. Clark compared his joy to the feeling described in Isaiah 35:5–6:

> Then will the eyes of the blind be opened
>   and the ears of the deaf unstopped.
> Then will the lame leap like a deer,
>   and the mute tongue shout for joy.

Though his next two surgeries were unsuccessful, Clark realized that God would teach him through those failures. Failure, he believed, should be a friend, because it forces us to stop and think before we proceed. Often success comes as we pray and consider options before us and adjust our plan of action.

Dr. Clark learned from his failures, and today his cochlear implant has helped many people. In his book, Dr. Clark wrote,

> When all deaf children can have the opportunity of hearing and learning to speak, my dream will come true. In 1970, when I was in a makeshift laboratory in the disused hospital mortuary, I could not have imagined that within thirty years, 14,000 children from more than fifty countries would have bene-fited from this tiny artifact, our bionic ear. Our Father in heaven, hallowed be your name.[1]

Jesus healed the deaf man who lived near the Sea of Galilee, and I'm convinced he still heals people today. But sometimes he uses the hands and hearts of committed men like Dr. Clark to heal us of our infirmities.

I now believe that a cochlear implant is the medical miracle for which I prayed when little John fell down. Before making a decision, I spoke to many people, asked a lot of questions, and researched the subject. In the spring of 2002, I told my husband, John, that I was ready to do it.

My surgeon, Dr. John Niparko, advised me to exercise three months before the surgery. So, to prepare, I walked and ran about two miles five days a week in addition to my ballet workout. Dr. Niparko believes that exercise helps patients recover faster, and it seems he was right. I left the hospital three hours after my surgery and even walked a mile with my husband that evening.

Sure, I had been nervous. For a full week before the August operation, I had butterflies in my stomach every night and couldn't fall asleep. On the night before the surgery, I lay awake staring into the darkness until 2 A.M. After only a couple hours of sleep, I woke up and turned to Bible reading. God always comforts me with his words.

At the hospital in Baltimore, my husband teased me about Dr. Niparko shaving my head; thank goodness, he had to shave only a small patch behind my ear. We prayed together for a safe surgery. Within a few minutes, the anesthetic took effect. Then after the surgery, when the anesthesia had completely worn off, John came into the room and helped me dress to leave the hospital.

Anyone who saw me on the street that day would never have known that my world had just been dramatically altered.

More Than My Imagination

The Nucleus device was activated on September 19, six weeks after my surgery. I had decided to allow *Good Morning America* to tape the activation because I want to do all I can to encourage others, particularly children, who might benefit from cochlear implants.

We flew to Baltimore to work with Dr. Niparko and his team, and John, the boys, my mother, and my mother-in-law were with me when I heard my first sound—the sound of Jennifer Yeagle, my audiologist, clapping her hands. At first I wondered if I was imagining the clapping sound. Then it hit me. *No, I'm not imagining this.* It was so much more crisp than the sound I received through my left-ear hearing aid. *It's real.* So real I had to cry.

I didn't hear everything at once, and Dr. Niparko assured me that listening is a process we develop over years. Except for what I absorbed through my hearing aid, I had not heard sounds since the Vietnam War.

I could not hear my boys' voices on that first day. But later that afternoon, as I changed clothes in a restroom, I shuffled through the makeup I carry in a small plastic case. To my amazement, I heard small clicking sounds as the makeup bottles tapped against each other. I was so startled, I forgot what I was looking for. I was so excited, I just stood there, moving things around for the joy of the sound.

A few minutes later, I pulled out a small can of hairspray. I pushed the button and heard a *ssss* sound. I was so surprised, I stared at the can and pushed the button again, just to be sure the button and the buzz were linked. Again and again I pushed the button, as delighted with a new sound as a child is with a new toy.

Later that day, I could hear people's voices a tiny bit, but I could not differentiate among them. And the voices were incredibly soft, so quiet it was frustrating to strain to hear them.

That first day, filled with media interviews, tired me out. I was grateful when John and I got back to our hotel where we could rest. As I got ready to go to bed early, not paying much attention to sounds, God surprised with the most beautiful sound I heard all day. As I turned on the water to brush my teeth, a beautiful, natural music danced in my ear. I recognized the rhythms in the sounds of dripping water. I could hear water with my hearing aid, but never before like this. Clear, crisp.

I turned the water on and off, listening and thinking of my role model, Helen Keller. The sound and feel of running water had triggered her understanding and opened the window to a new world. In *Light in My Darkness,* she wrote, "That word, water, dropped into my mind like the sun in a frozen winter world."[2] In some small measure I now shared her joy of discovery.

Children are the best candidates for cochlear implants because their brains are still "plastic" and can easily assimilate new information. Helen Keller was an older child when she first learned the word *water.* It will be harder for me, as an adult, to learn new sounds, but I will think of Helen and draw inspiration from her example.

That night as I lay in bed, I heard God's voice speak to my heart: "Heather, I will bless you with a new gift of sound every day. You will hear your boys at the right time because I love you."

And that's how I see today and tomorrow and however many more days of life I am privileged to possess: Each day is a gift of God, each sound a blessing I don't deserve. God is so good!

On the second day with my cochlear implant, John, the boys, and I took a tour of Capitol Hill. We were walking on the sidewalk outside the magnificent Capitol Building when I heard the sounds of my footsteps on the pavement. I also heard the sound of the breeze blowing my hair, and I felt God's presence near. In that moment, I thanked God that he did not allow me to hear all the new sounds at once. Doing it this way, I could savor a new sound before moving on to the next. I know each day of the next six months will be like Christmas. I will be able to open a delightful gift each day.

On the third day, I heard my first word—"yup." We were on an airplane watching a movie. I did not hear the music or many voices, but I heard a character say "yup" perfectly and clearly. Again I thought I was imagining the sound, so I turned to John and said, "I think I heard the word *yup*."

John said, "You mean, you heard *yup?*"

And when John said it, I heard it again. When I said, "Yes, I heard it." I suddenly could hear my own voice better than before. In the airplane, I heard the flight attendants close the overhead compartments. I heard the zipper on my purse. And the sounds of other people's voices, while still fuzzy, were becoming clearer.

I know it will take some time before I learn how to process so many new sounds. The Bible tells us that when Jesus healed the deaf mute, immediately the man's ears were opened and he began to "speak plainly." That is truly a miracle from God, because most deaf people who have their hearing restored must learn how to speak and how to listen. We have to learn how to sort through the thousands of sounds that will enter our ears and clamor for our attention.

When you have been living in a silent world, entering the noisy world can be a jarring experience. Before the event, Dr. Niparko explained that when he turned on my cochlear implant, it would be like hearing the noises of a Russian town. I would hear all sorts of sounds, but they would be unfamiliar so I wouldn't understand. He said it would take me anywhere from two to five years to learn to identify all the new sounds.

MY SON'S VOICE!

As I write this, nearly a month after the activation of my cochlear implant, I am thrilled to say that I can hear my boys' voices. They are still indistinct—maybe like when you watch television and the volume is turned too low.

The first time I heard them, I was driving. When I *thought* I heard James's voice, I glanced around and saw him fussing, because he wanted to get out of his car seat. Even with a fussy baby, that was a wonderful moment!

And October 22, 2002, was a red-letter day. A few days before, I had bought a child-sized music player and two microphones for the boys. Because I could not yet hear them clearly and I did not want to turn up the volume of the Nucleus device, I hoped I would hear them better if they talked into the microphones.

Well, they absolutely loved being stars. They talked a lot into the microphones and sang along to the music. I could hear them a bit better, but their voices were still low and fuzzy.

Later that day John-John played the audio cassette for one of the boys' favorite books, *Goodnight Moon.* He listened carefully the first time, then, when we played it again, he repeated the sweet words into the microphone after the reader said them.

I heard his soft voice and understood perfectly when he said, "Goodnight, moon." Those precious words, which have sent many a baby to dreamland, were the first words I understood from his mouth.

All four of us celebrated that night. Sometimes children are our best teachers.

Though I still cannot understand most of what my boys say, I know my brain is involved in the process of learning to decipher their voices. It is a challenge and sometimes frustrating, but I am grateful for the sounds.

Because of my position as a former Miss America, my implant received a lot of publicity—an article in *People Magazine,* television appearances, and many interviews. Though the weeks following my activation were hectic, I wanted to do what I could to help spread the word about the miracle God has enabled surgeons like Dr. Niparko to perform. After my surgery, I received many letters from people who had received cochlear implants. They told me that hearing would present many challenges at the beginning. One man said he hadn't heard a sound for three months. My right ear hadn't heard anything in twenty-eight years, so I knew it was unrealistic for me to hear a voice right away.

I'm still learning to identify sounds that hearing people take for granted. For several months I'll be working with a therapist who will help me deal with unfamiliar sounds and devise new communication strategies. I know that in time, I will learn to identify all the sounds that hearing people take for granted.

S P R E A D I N G   T H E   H E A L I N G   W O R D

Jesus worked a great miracle when he healed the man who could not hear or speak. At first I identified with the deaf man, but now I'm beginning to identify with the wonderful people who brought the man to Jesus. Not only did they care enough to seek help for their friend, but afterward they cared enough to tell others that yes, there is a Healer and his name is Jesus!

That's why I love to talk about my Lord. I also love to talk about the wonderful people who are working to help heal deaf children. In the six years since I became Miss America, I have received letters from those who have relationships with deaf children. They often feel depressed and tell me that it is unfair that their children have to struggle to achieve their dreams. Often deaf children are teased by other children without disabilities.

I'll be honest—those letters often made me feel as frustrated as the parents who wrote me. Like them, I wanted to deliver their children and spare them pain, but there was nothing I could do. I don't have the power to heal deafness or stop other teasing children.

It is important that deaf children learn to function in the healing world. Between the ages of eleven through fourteen, I attended a boarding school for deaf children, Central Institute for the Deaf. I had many friends and for the first time in my life, I felt I was a part of conversations around a dinner table. But this sweet world was unrealistic. That's why CID only teaches students until age fourteen; after that we are encouraged to attend hearing schools to learn to make our way in the world.

When I was in high school, I missed my friends from CID. I had few friends in my hearing high school because few people took the time to talk to me. I felt left out, but at least I had my dance, my books, and my family to turn to. They were my safety net.

I don't want other deaf children to endure what I went through. With the support of Cochlear Americas, I will soon embrace Dr. Graeme Clark's dream of helping all deaf children to hear. Along with their team, I will educate the public about the opportunities cochlear implants provide profoundly deaf individuals, especially those who cannot hear with hearing aids.

This means I will be traveling, but no more than five days a month because I want to be home with my boys. Being a mom is my number one priority right now. Thanks to a medical miracle and the goodness of God, I will soon be able to hear their laughter—and I'll hear them when they call out for help.

Our God is a God of healing. Sometimes he heals through miracles, sometimes he heals through medicine, and sometimes he heals through both. Let God surprise you—pray for guidance, then walk through the doors he opens for you.

What did Jesus tell the man who could not hear or speak? "Be opened!"

In what ways can you open yourself to the Lord's leadership? Let God surprise you with physical, emotional, or spiritual healing!

fourteen

SURPRISED BY FORGIVENESS

∽

ONE RECENT AFTERNOON I DESPERATELY NEEDED A NAP TO restore my energy. My two young boys are a handful, and they demand my attention every moment of the day. When a mother has two toddlers less than a year apart, she tends to collapse on occasion because she is not God! After being the mom of two young boys for two years, I have a greater admiration for God who gives his children constant attention.

On this afternoon not long after the activation of my cochlear implant, I was completely drained. James, my younger, went right to sleep, but John-John did not want to nap even though he was sleepy. I put him on his bed, then went into my bedroom and lay down.

Through my hearing aid I could hear John-John fussing from his bedroom, but I closed my eyes tighter and ignored him. Then he was quiet. Relieved, I thought he had gone to sleep. I was just about to drop into a doze when I heard someone whisper "Mommy" in a quiet voice.

I silently prayed, "Please, Lord, let this be a dream." I kept my eyes closed.

Then I heard "Mommy" again. I opened my eyes and there stood little John, his face only inches away from mine. He was smiling and holding the *People* magazine that featured a picture of him helping me put the cochlear implant device on my ear.

Proudly, he pointed to his picture. "I am Dr. McCallum," he said, "because I help Mommy to hear."

My heart melted. A moment before I had been wanting to say, "Lord, please don't tell me that my new hearing will mean that I'll lose even more sleep," but how could I think that when I looked at my son's proud face?

I drew him into my arms and hugged him, happy to forgive him for disturbing my rest.

This is just a small illustration of our need to extend and receive forgiveness. In this chapter I want to show you scenes of forgiveness that are far more serious, beginning with Jesus' forgiveness of his friend Peter.

IMPETUOUS, IRREPRESSIBLE PETER

Shortly after Jesus began his public ministry, a fisherman named Andrew left his work site and followed Jesus. The first thing he did was tell his older brother Simon his good news: "We have found the Messiah" (John 1:41).

Later, Jesus welcomed Simon in a most unusual way—by changing his name. "Jesus looked at him and said, 'You are Simon son of John. You will be called Cephas' (which, when translated is Peter)" (John 1:42). What does Peter mean? In Greek *petros* means a "rock detached from the living rock."

Peter and Andrew and their fisherman cousins James and John were rough-hewn Galileans. Having received the religious training given to all young Jewish men, they were familiar with Scriptures and the prophecies about the coming Messiah. But unlike Paul, whom we considered in a previous chapter, they hadn't advanced to higher studies of the law under the personal tutorship of the rabbis.

Jesus quickly chose Simon Peter to become one of his disciples—fishers of men, as the Gospel describes them (Matt. 4:19). He traveled with Jesus and witnessed many mind-boggling miracles, including Jesus' calming the storm and feeding five thousand people with five fish and two loaves of bread. He saw Moses and Elijah appear with Jesus at the Transfiguration. Peter even walked on water with the Lord!

Peter had every reason to believe Jesus was the son of God—and not a single reason to doubt. He did not hesitate to proclaim Jesus' identity: "You are the Christ, the Son of the living God" (Matt. 16:16).

In many sermons about Peter's shameful denial of Jesus, he is portrayed as a complete coward. I'd like you to look at Peter in another light. Years ago evangelist Grady Nutt used this illustration, and the truth of it has stuck with me. I think this new perspective may help you look at Peter through new eyes.

Look at Peter not as the disciple-turned-coward, but as Barney Fife. That's right, Sheriff Andy Taylor's (Andy Griffith's) sidekick in Mayberry, North Carolina. One-bullet Deputy Fife, the man who was so skittish Andy made him carry an unloaded gun with one bullet safely tucked into his shirt pocket.

With that analogy in mind, let's look at highlights of Peter's story, beginning with a day when Jesus tries to explain the path his life would take. Peter didn't want to listen.

> Jesus began to explain to his disciples that he must go to Jerusalem and suffer many things at the hands of the elders, chief priests and teachers of the law, and that he must be killed and on the third day be raised to life.
>
> Peter took him aside and began to rebuke him. "Never, Lord!" he said. "This shall never happen to you!"
>
> Jesus turned and said to Peter, "Get behind me, Satan! You are a stumbling block to me; you do not have in mind the things of God, but the things of men" (Matt. 16:21–23).

A faithful deputy, Peter wasn't going to let this happen to his Lord. No, not if he could help it.

But weeks later, reality began to unfold at the spring Passover feast. After sharing the Passover meal with his disciples, Jesus walked with them to the Mount of Olives, where he quietly announced that all the disciples would "fall away"—scatter like sheep. Again, loyal Peter contradicted him.

Peter declared, "Even if all fall away, I will not."

"I tell you the truth," Jesus answered, "today—yes, tonight—before the rooster crows twice you yourself will disown me three times."

But Peter insisted emphatically, "Even if I have to die with you, I will never disown you." And all the others said the same (Mark 14:29–31).

After this exchange, Jesus took Peter, James, and John further into the garden of Gethsemane to pray. Later in the night Judas crashed the scene with soldiers and officials from the chief priests. I can see Peter tensing up, his hand fumbling for his bullet—I mean, his sword.

Judas approached Jesus, to betray him with a kiss. A soldier moved in to take Jesus captive. Observing the threat, Peter leapt forward to defend his Lord. He flashed the sword from his belt and sliced off the ear of a servant named Malchus (John 18:10).

Rebuking Peter, Jesus gently restored the ear.

Does Peter seem like a coward in this scene? He looks more like an over-eager Barney Fife to me! And consider this: Matthew 26:56 says that at that moment "all the disciples deserted him and fled." Barney—I mean, Peter—jumped the gun, but the other disciples fled! John, James, Andrew, Philip, Matthew, Levi, and all the others turned tail and ran without lifting a finger to defend Jesus, who was bound and led to the home of the high priest.

But the night was still young. While Judas collected his blood money and nine of the disciples cowered in hiding, two doubled back to reconnoiter—Peter and his cousin John, who was on speaking terms with someone in the high priest's household. As the book of John states, "Simon Peter and another disciple were following Jesus. Because this disciple [John] was known to the high priest, he went with Jesus into the high priest's courtyard, but Peter had to wait outside at the door" (John 18:15–16).

So while John followed Jesus into the compound to meet with the high priest, Barney—I mean Peter—squatted outside the gate, warming his hands and trying to look nonchalant. Don't you know his head was spinning with ideas! Was there a way to bust Jesus out of the house? Hard to do with only two loyal men here. But maybe he could count on others, friends in high places. Maybe Nicodemus. Maybe Joseph of Arimathea. Peter didn't know what he was doing, but he desperately wanted to do *something*. I'm sure he told himself that he wasn't a coward. He was a good man, devoted and loyal, a man who was convinced his master would not suffer and die on *his* watch.

While Peter was trying to come up with a plan, a serving girl noticed his roughshod appearance. Galileans from the north were less genteel and polished than Jerusalem natives. He was not exactly the sort of man who regularly visited the posh home of the high priest. Plus, she had been out and about in town and had seen Peter in Jesus' company. She was an eyewitness, and Barney's—I mean Peter's—cover was blown. "But [Peter] denied it before them all. 'I don't know what you're talking about,' he said" (Matthew 26:70).

Just after Peter made this blustering announcement, John came to the gate and gestured for Peter to come inside.

Whew! Peter was saved from an embarrassing situation in the nick of time. But even though he was now in the entry of the house, he was still not close to the Lord. Secret Agent Fife was still fumbling, still bumbling, still moving forward without any clear plan.

And other people kept getting in the way.

> Then he went out to the gateway, where another girl saw him and said to the people there, "This fellow was with Jesus of Nazareth."
> He denied it again, with an oath: "I don't know the man!" (Matt. 26:71–72)

Peter was getting a little testy. Barney Fife would have to be hard-pressed to resort to undercover swearing, yet Peter let loose, hoping a little forceful language would augment his disguise.

To get closer to the situation, Peter moved to the fire in the center of the area, mingling with guards and officials who had ambushed Jesus in Gethsemane. But nobody bought his act.

> After a little while, those standing there went up to Peter and said, "Surely you are one of them, for your accent gives you away."
> Then he began to call down curses on himself and he swore to them, "I don't know the man!" (Matt. 26:73–74)

Barney—I mean Peter—was riled! Nothing was going right. His cover was blown. The scent of blood filled the air; it wouldn't take much for those people to look for other scapegoats. Peter was penned, caught like a rabbit in a snare. He cursed himself. He cursed everything in sight. He swore that he knew nothing about Jesus.

Right then, just when he was considering a run for the gate, a rooster crowed, announcing a new day. Peter looked up in time to see the guards lead Jesus out of the interrogation room.

And immediately, the Lord turned and looked straight at Peter. "Then Peter remembered the word the Lord had spoken to him" (Luke 22:61). *Peter, before dawn you will disown me.* Seeing acknowledgment, pain, and love in Jesus' brown eyes, Peter went outside and "wept bitterly" (22:62).

Two men committed grievous acts of betrayal that night—Judas, who sold his master for thirty pieces of silver, and Peter, who publicly denied even knowing the Lord. But there is a major difference in the outcomes of the two stories. Faced with what he had done, Judas went out and committed suicide. When Peter looked upon the loving face of Jesus, the impetuous fisherman wept in broken repentance.

We don't know that Peter was present at the crucifixion, but surely he quickly heard reports of Jesus' dying words, forgiving the repentant thief and even the people responsible for his death. "Father, forgive them, for they do not know what they are doing" (Luke 23:34). Peter was able to accept those words personally. And in accepting Christ's forgiveness, he was able to forgive himself and face Jesus confidently at a later seaside meeting.

Through Jesus' love and God's power, God honored Peter after Jesus' resurrection. Just as Andy Taylor made allowances for Barney's blunders, Jesus took pains to show Peter that he was forgiven. He had been a reed, easily blown about by the winds of turmoil, but he would become a rock, a part of the living stone.

Scripture later records a significant encounter between Peter and the risen Lord. Peter was fishing with some of the other disciples and when someone told him Jesus was standing on the bank, Peter did not run away in embarrassment and shame. Rather, he leapt into the water and swam to shore to greet him.

After the group had eaten a fish breakfast together, Jesus addressed Peter directly:

> "Simon son of John, do you truly love me more than these?"
>
> "Yes, Lord," he said, "you know that I love you."
>
> Jesus said, "Feed my lambs."
>
> Again Jesus said, "Simon son of John, do you truly love me?"
>
> He answered, "Yes, Lord, you know that I love you."
>
> Jesus said, "Take care of my sheep."
>
> The third time he said to him, "Simon son of John, do you love me?"
>
> Peter was hurt because Jesus asked him the third time, "Do you love me?" He said, "Lord, you know all things; you know that I love you."
>
> Jesus said, "Feed my sheep. . . ." Then he said to him, "Follow me!" (John 21:15–19)

Peter, who had denied Jesus three times, was now asked to confirm his love for Jesus three times. Though we do not know the exact details of Peter's death (tradition holds that he was crucified upside down because he said he was not worthy to die like the Lord), his life exemplified devotion to the Lord. Peter was indeed the rock, and he fulfilled the prophecy Jesus had made earlier: "You are Peter, and on this rock I will build my church, and the gates of Hades will not overcome it. I will give you the keys of the kingdom of heaven; whatever you bind on earth will be bound in heaven, and whatever you loose on earth will be loosed in heaven" (Matt. 16:18–19).

Peter "opened the doors" of faith to three separate groups: the Jews, to whom he preached at Pentecost (Acts 2:38); the Samaritans (8:14–17); and the Gentiles, whom he addressed at the home of Cornelius (10:44). On each occasion, after Peter preached the news of Jesus' death and resurrection, the Holy Spirit descended, giving evidence that salvation was meant for *everyone*.

Jesus forgave Peter. And no matter how you have failed, Jesus will forgive you too. When we fail, in large ways or small, we can claim the same mercy Peter sought.

FORGIVING AT MANY LEVELS

God's forgiveness of our sin is only half the story. As children forgiven by God, we are asked to extend that forgiveness to others. Jesus said, "And when you stand praying, if you hold anything against anyone, forgive him, so that your Father in heaven may forgive you your sins" (Mark 11:25).

In her dramatic book *Forgiving the Dead Man Walking,* Debbie Morris shows how forgiveness is a process or journey, sometimes with unexpected turns.

One summer night in 1980, sixteen-year-old Debbie Cuevas and her boyfriend, Mark Brewster, were sitting in his car drinking milkshakes. Two men approached, and before Debbie and Mark could react, the men pulled out guns and got in the vehicle. Telling Debbie and Mark they wanted only the car and money, they drove the teenagers from Louisiana to Alabama, where they pulled Mark out of the car, tortured him, shot him, and left him in the woods to die. Then, with Debbie, they drove back to Louisiana, where they repeatedly raped her. She spent more than thirty hours with her captors before she was able to get away. Even more terrifying were the hints she picked up, leading her to believe they had murdered another girl only three days earlier.

The two kidnappers, Robert Willie and Joseph Vaccaro, were caught, tried, and imprisoned. Willie was sentenced to death. The book and movie *Dead Man Walking* is based in part on Willie's story and the in-prison ministry of Sister Helen Prejean.

The night Willie was scheduled for execution, Debbie, at home in bed, took a first step toward forgiving him. In prayer she turned to God.

> "Lord, please help me deal with whatever happens tonight. I really do forgive Robert Willie. As best I can anyway ..."
>
> With that prayer pronouncing my forgiveness on Robert Willie, I gained an emotional release....

It cut me loose from the control [he] had over me for all those years.[1]

But even then, Debbie was not at peace.

Because of the rape, I felt like damaged goods. I always thought people would look at me and see the faces of Robert Willie and Joseph Vaccaro, think about what they did to me, then instantly be disgusted by me. . . .

I also suffered from depression. I lashed out at family members and started drinking, despite everything I knew about alcoholism, about how it devastates families. My drinking dulled the pain.[2]

Eight years after the crime, she checked herself into a thirty-day treatment program, where the counselors helped her identify suppressed anger and resentment. Debbie says, "That eventually forced me to admit something I'd tried for years not to think about: an awful lot of my anger and resentment was directed at God."[3]

"I felt abandoned by God," Debbie admits. She had accepted Christ as a fourteen-year-old at a church camp, but felt he had left her alone during her kidnapping ordeal and its aftermath. "It took me years to realize I'd abandoned him."[4]

Years passed. Debbie had married, become a school teacher, and begun to look forward to the birth of her first child when the book *Forgiving the Dead Man Walking* was released. Tensions mounted, partly because of the increased publicity and partly because the book seemed sympathetic to Willie. More than a year later, Debbie learned about the movie starring Susan Sarandon and Sean Penn. "As upset as I'd been to learn about the book, this was worse."[5]

Finally Debbie realized no one but God could handle her tumultuous emotions, and in time she saw how very present he *had* been in her great ordeal.

> Not only had God been with me at my lowest, most desperate moments, he had uniquely equipped me to survive everything I'd been through. . . .
>
> Instead of complaining and asking God why he hadn't solved my problems, I began asking God what he wanted me to do and how he wanted to use the circumstances and experiences of my life.[6]

But something held her back. In time she came to understand that she was unable to discover or carry out what God planned for her life. Debbie says,

> [This was] because I had never been able to forgive the most central character in my personal drama. I'd forgiven Robert Willie and Joseph Vaccaro as best I could. . . . I had even reached the point where I'd forgiven God. But I had not yet forgiven myself.
>
> I realized that before I could do that, I had to feel that God had forgiven me. Which in turn meant I needed to ask his forgiveness. . . .
>
> As I came to know and feel God's forgiveness, it was suddenly easy to forgive myself.[7]

What brought Debbie to a place of peace and more complete forgiveness of Willie? She says it was a simple, profound realization:

I needed to accept a difficult truth: God loved Robert Willie as much as he loves me. Jesus' parable about the vineyard workers in Matthew 20 finally put this into perspective for me. A few years ago, I applied it to Robert Willie and realized it didn't matter how late in the game he came to Jesus, as long as he came. And if he did, God wanted him every bit as much as he wants me.

This has been the final step in my forgiveness.[8]

BOUNDLESS FORGIVENESS, MATCHLESS GRACE

While visiting in the home of Simon—not Simon Peter, but a wealthy Pharisee—Jesus told the following story:

> "Two men owed money to a certain moneylender. One owed him five hundred denarii, and the other fifty. Neither of them had the money to pay him back, so he canceled the debts of both. Now which of them will love him more?"
>
> Simon replied, "I suppose the one who had the bigger debt canceled."
>
> "You have judged correctly," Jesus said.
>
> Then he turned toward the woman and said to Simon, "Do you see this woman? I came into your house. You did not give me any water for my feet, but she wet my feet with her tears and wiped them with her hair. You did not give me a kiss, but this woman, from the time I entered, has not stopped kissing my feet. You did not put oil on my head, but she has poured perfume on my feet. Therefore, I tell you, her many sins have been forgiven—for she loved much. But he who has been forgiven little loves little" (Luke 7:41–47).

Tradition holds that the woman who washed Jesus' feet with her tears was a prostitute. Simon, who prided himself on his good works and spiritual knowledge, couldn't begin to match the woman's passionate love for the Savior.

Have you been forgiven from the wrongs you have committed? No one, not even a philanthropist, lives a perfect life. At the core, our natures are all-too human, too driven to envy, greed, and pride. There are times when the Spirit of God pricks my conscience, and I am horrified by the selfishness in my own life. Yet my sin is the basis of my love for God. How could I not love the one who forgave so much?

When I look at those who hurt me, I cannot help but think of how richly my life has been saturated with forgiveness. And when I extend my hand in mercy, the sweet aroma of God's grace wafts over those around me, and they are blessed too.

If a secret sin haunts your life, confess it today—and be surprised by the incredible wealth of God's forgiveness.

If you have withheld forgiveness in order to nurse an old wound, know that you can find healing and release in that same wealth.

Finally, if there is some sin you cannot forgive yourself, remember that if God can forgive, so can you. After all, he is God!

Forgive—and let God surprise you with his amazing love!

NOTES

CHAPTER 1: SURPRISED BY BIG DREAMS

1. William Federer, *America's God and Country Encyclopedia of Quotations* (USA: Fame, 1996), 96.

2. Ibid., 95.

3. Ibid., 96.

CHAPTER 2: SURPRISED BY SIN

1. "Eve," *Easton's 1987 Bible Dictionary* on CD.

2. Stephen Arterburn and Angela Hunt, *Flashpoints* (Wheaton, IL: Tyndale, 2002), 13.

3. Ibid.

CHAPTER 3: SURPRISED BY NEW FAITH

1. William Federer, *America's God and Country Encyclopedia of Quotations* (USA: Fame, 1996), 523.

2. Ibid.

CHAPTER 4: SURPRISED BY ADVERSITY

1. Helen Keller, *Light in My Darkness* (West Chester, PA: Chrysalis, 1994), 12.

2. Ibid., 25.

3. Helen Keller, *Midstream, My Later Life* (Garden City, NY: Doubleday, 1929), 97.

CHAPTER 5: SURPRISED BY DELIVERANCE

1. Shelia Poole, "A Family Value," *The Atlanta Journal-Constitution* (29 May 2002): E1.

2. Editors of American Heritage, *The American Heritage Pictorial History of the Presidents of the United States* (n.p: American Heritage, 1968), 419.

3. F. B. Carpenter, *Harper's Weekly* (27 April 1867).

4. William Federer, *America's God and Country Encyclopedia of Quotations* (USA: Fame, 1996), 381–82.

5. Ibid., 389–90.

6. Ibid., 391.

7. Ibid.

CHAPTER 6: SURPRISED BY LOVE

1. William Petersen, *25 Surprising Marriages* (Grand Rapids: Baker, 1997), 154.

2. Ibid., 158.

3. Ibid., 151.

4. Ibid., 158.

5. Ibid., 163.

6. Ibid., 164.

CHAPTER 7: SURPRISED BY CHILDREN

1. Mark Water, comp., *The New Encyclopedia of Christian Quotations* (Grand Rapids: Baker, 2000), 351.

2. Review, "Holding on to Hope," *Publishers Weekly* (27 May 2002): 56.

3. Nancy Guthrie, *Holding On To Hope* (Wheaton, IL: Tyndale, 2002), 24–25.

4. Ibid., 65.

5. Kristin Billerbeck's story, personal correspondence with Angela Hunt, June 2002.

6. Deborah Raney, personal correspondence with Angela Hunt, June 2002.

7. Quoted in Miriam Huffman Rockness, *Keep These Things, Ponder Them in Your Heart* (New York: Doubleday, 1979), 32.

CHAPTER 8: SURPRISED BY PROVISION

1. Corrie ten Boom, with John and Elizabeth Sherrill, *The Hiding Place* (New York: Bantam, 1975), 193.

2. Ibid., 202.

CHAPTER 9: SURPRISED BY MINISTRY

1. Jim McNutt, *A Single Journey* (Ann Arbor: Servant, 1998), 227.

2. Lowell "Bud" Paxon, *Threading the Needle* (New York: Harper Business, 1998), 3.

3. Ibid., 87.

4. Ibid., 92.

5. Ibid., 93.

6. Ibid., 18.

7. Ibid., 110.

8. Ibid., 25.

Chapter 10: Surprised by Conflict

1. Quoted in John Pollock, *William Wilberforce* (Burke, VA: Trinity Forum, 1996), 14.

2. Ibid., 16.

3. Ibid.

4. Ibid., 12.

5. Interview with Kevin Belmonte, *www.gordon.edu/ccs/CBD_interview.html,* accessed 23 January 2003.

Chapter 11: Surprised by Angels

1. Mark Andrew Ritchie, *Spirit of the Rainforest* (Chicago: Island Lake, 1989), 122.

2. Joni Eareckson Tada, *Heaven* (Grand Rapids: Zondervan, 1995), 83.

3. Ibid., 84.

4. Ritchie, *Spirit of the Rainforest*, 206.

5. Ibid.

6. Henry Ward Beecher, *Royal Truths,* quoted in Frank Mead, *The Encyclopedia of Religious Quotations* (Old Tappan, NJ: Revell, 1965), 5.

Chapter 13: Surprised by Healing

1. Graeme Clark, *Sounds from Silence* (St. Leonards, Australia: Allen and Unwin, 2000), 190.

2. Helen Keller, *Light in My Darkness, Light in My Darkness* (West Chester, PA: Chrysalis, 1994), 18.

Chapter 14: Surprised by Forgiveness

1. Debbie Morris with Gregg Lewis, *Forgiving the Dead Man Walking* (Grand Rapids: Zondervan, 1998), 173.

2. Jane Johnson Struck, "Forgiving the Dead Man Walking," *www.christianity today.com/tcw/9w3/9w3022.html,* accessed 23 January 2003.

3. Morris, *Forgiving the Dead Man Walking*, 188.

4. Struck, "Forgiving the Dead Man Walking."

5. Morris, *Forgiving the Dead Man Walking*, 217.

6. Ibid., 222–23.

7. Ibid., 223–24.

8. Struck, "Forgiving the Dead Man Walking."